**ISBN:** 9798835421534
**Imprint:** Independently published
**First published 2023**

A legal deposit copy of this book has been s

With so much love and gratitude to the many wonderful humans who have helped and supported me in bringing this book to fruition.

Thank you to my boys for being my raison d'etre, always, to Leo, Mum, Dad & Aimee for your tireless love and support, to Kym for your deep friendship through hard times and good, to Jairek and Amanda for showing me the kind of coach and person I strive to be, to Charlotte Popple who helped me get started and the BWi women who helped me get finished, to every wonderful rushing woman who has trusted me and taken part in this course, and to every rushing woman who has not yet discovered it, this book is for you. And, to my husband Adam, gone from my sight but never far from my soul.

Thursday, Thursday…. what it is I haven't done?

Both kids in school? Check

Both got lunch? Yes.

PE stuff? Yes.

It's not swimming today. No.

Bin day? No, it's not that.

The sound of my mobile vibrating on the table in front of me brings me back into the conference room. John's on slide 19 of a 20 slide deck. I glance down at my 'phone. It's my mother in law calling. Lunch break is scheduled in 10 minutes, I'll call her back. I'm presenting after lunch. I was up until midnight prepping. What have I forgotten?

"Thank you John. Lunch everyone, see you back here at 1.15pm".

Everyone files out, making for the café or the lavatories or milling about in the corridor as I fumble to dial mother in law on the 'phone.

"Hi, sorry, I missed a call from you…….."

I watched as my mobile 'phone fell away from me in slow motion, toward the rough blue grey carpet tiles of the corridor. I'd lost all peripheral vision but I could hear the noises around me. I heard a strange, guttural bellow, a sort of bovine sound. I realised it had come from me.

"Ellen?…….Ellen? What's ……" I still couldn't see anything except the carpet at my feet, but I was aware of a kind colleague rushing toward me. As I felt her at my elbow my knees turned to jelly and gave way beneath me. She supported me over to a sofa and with composure that seemed astonishing to me in my distress, asked the confused looking couple who had been eating lunch there to please move.

I remember climbing onto the sofa on my hands and knees. I've no idea why.

"My husband's committed[1] suicide in the garage" I managed.

"What?"

"My husband's committed suicide in the garage".

---

[1] I've since learned a lot and no longer say 'committed' but 'died by'; a distinction very important to me, and I believe to a great many others. But I did not know that then.

# Chapter One. Where are you now?

Hi Ellen,

I'm wondering whether this is something you can help with. Two years ago I was made redundant and so I took the plunge to start my own business! It's been a rocky road but I'm starting to see real progress, it's growing and I have some regular retainer clients as well as ad hoc bits, I'm pleased with the growth in turnover, it's not where I want it to be yet, but it's heading in the right direction. However, to achieve this I'm getting about three hours sleep a night at the moment. I'm working all hours. I want to make my business work for me, but I've realised I also feel as if I have a point to prove to my family, I want them to see it be a success and I know I'm pushing myself hard.

I know I'm missing out on time with my kids, which makes me feel guilty; they're teens and I know they won't be at home forever. I'm gaining weight I want to lose but there's no way I'm going to fit in exercise at the moment even though I really want to and I'm feeling really resentful that it's me doing absolutely everything at home too. My husband works long days and I don't want to put upon him by asking him to help more at home, I feel I should be able to do it.

I felt I had to reach out because I know that actually, I'm really struggling. Is this the kind of thing you can help with?

Melissa

What made you pick up this book? Something made you think this might be a book you need. Perhaps you're feeling a bit like Melissa? Is overwhelm showing up in your life at the moment? How is busy-ness impacting you?

Tell me if any of this sounds familiar;

- You feel wound up like a coiled spring
- You run yourself ragged in a daily battle to keep up
- There is always so much to do and you rarely feel as if you are in control or get on top of things
- You often feel overwhelmed
- You feel anxious easily
- You find your breathing tends to be shallow and quite fast
- Everything seems urgent
- You find it hard to say no, and feel guilty when you do
- You find it hard to ask for help

I've heard the above list many, many times when women first come to start work with me; women like Melissa, women juggling a burgeoning career or their own growing business with a growing family, trying to nurture a relationship with their spouse and feeling that part of themselves has been 'lost' along the way. They don't laugh as much as they used to and they often have trouble sleeping. They find it very difficult to switch off and relax.

I'm here to tell you, firstly, you're not imagining it! You're not 'being silly', 'blowing it out of proportion' or 'just letting things get on top of you'. That stress you feel is real. There are likely to be real biochemical changes going on in your body that are contributing to you feeling this way; it's in your body as well as your mind. Stress isn't a choice, it's a state and you can't just 'look on the bright side' or 'pull your socks up'. There are a lot of helpful techniques for dealing with feeling stressed in body and mind, we'll look at some of these in this book but importantly, we're going to address the underlying cause, not just how to control the symptoms.

A large part of the trouble, I believe, is that we've been led to accept that this is just the way 21$^{st}$ century life is. I've heard many women say it; "I'm just going to have to accept that this is the way life is. Life is just going to be this busy until......" That is another part of the problem. The until. We're all looking to some future date once the children are older or once they've left home, or once I've got enough money, or once I've lost that weight. We're all waiting for this magical time in the future when it will be easier to be calmer, when things will slow down a bit and be less rushed and less pressured. There are several problems with this approach. One is that if we keep taking each day on its own merits and just reacting to the huge amounts of information coming at us each day and don't take back control of our time, we will find that we are ever so busy treading water. Exhaustingly busy all the time, yet feeling as if we're getting nowhere. If you want things to be different, you have to do things differently and do different things. Waiting for that magic 'one day when things are calmer' is not going to work. It's you who has to change the way you're doing things.

Another problem with this approach is that, sadly, for some people that 'one day' never arrives. The death of my husband was a stark reminder of that for me, and an important impetus to make me determined to live the life I love each and everyday, not some day in the future. Let's not put up with the overwhelm, the busy-ness, the rush, the everything feels urgent, the lack of sleep, the lack of quality time with the people we love most, because we're waiting for this 'some day' when things are less hectic. Unexpected things happen in life, things you couldn't possibly have foreseen. Sometimes that 'one day when things slow down a bit' that you're working so hard to reach, doesn't come. This book shows you how to implement a method that helps you to enjoy the life you love everyday, not someday. The Method to Take Back Your Time; it's not one more thing to do, it's the way of getting things done.

I talk to many women who feel their lives are just so busy that they feel totally out of control. I hear all the time comments ranging from "I just need to get myself more organised" to "my sanity is hanging on by a frazzled thread". How did we get here? How did we get into this condition of being constantly stressed out, overly busy and rushed off our feet in a daily battle against the clock? Over the past 30 years or so we've seen faster, more dramatic changes in our lifestyles than we've seen for thousands and thousands of years before. Previously, change continued at a pretty steady and gradual pace and the chemistry in our bodies was able to keep up. However, since the industrial revolution in the 19th century, lifestyle change began to quicken as processes were mechanised. The past 30 years have seen even faster changes. We now have the Internet and mobile phones in our lives. If we're not very careful to set boundaries, we can find ourselves on call 24/7 with the buzzing, ringing, dinging, pinging of voicemails, emails, social media alerts going off on several devices around the house, day and night. We no longer leave work at work, and we can't assume that if we're at home we're spending time with our loved ones or on our own leisure activities. Often although we're at home, we cannot switch off our busy business brain, and frequently our body and our mind are not in the same place. You may be physically present at home with your family, but how many times do you find your mind wandering back to work, back to that unfinished To Do List, back to those meetings that you have tomorrow, things you have to prepare for, things you haven't had time to finish today, things that keep you awake at night. To make matters worse, we can sometimes be our own harshest critic. When it comes to home making tasks, much of our distress comes not from the unfolded laundry, the unmade bed or the dirty dishes in the sink, but from the stories we tell ourselves about it; that we must be lazy, a failure, not good enough because we're struggling to keep up. As K.C. Davis remarks in her book How to Keep House While Drowning, "In our society where homemaking tasks have historically been left to women, whilst the roles of daughter, wife and mother have widened to allow for ambition, career and equal partnership in the working world, the pattern of placing the main responsibility for the family's care or taking care of the home still frequently remains with the woman". We're taking on what would, historically, have been thought of as the work of our father or husband, as well as keeping the work traditionally assigned to women too. It's little wonder we're struggling with the juggling!

We're at our most fulfilled, peaceful and present when our mind and our body are both in the same place. But in this day and age, that can actually be surprisingly difficult to achieve; do you agree? The current pace of life with what feels like constant rush, stress, urgency and multitasking is pushing women more and more into a state where their nervous systems, reproductive systems and digestive systems are suffering as well as their emotional wellbeing[2].

There are several body systems involved in the busy woman's hurried lifestyle.

They include:

- The nervous system,
- The endocrine system, which includes the adrenal glands, ovaries, thyroid gland and pituitary gland.
- The digestive system.

Any or all of these may be affected by a hurried lifestyle. When you address just one of these systems, you might feel a little better. However, if the crazy busy, rushed lifestyle continues, your overall health is likely to continue to suffer.

Do you often feel tired but wired?

Made up of various body parts including your brain, your spinal cord and the nerves that connect your brain to every organ of your body, there are several components to the nervous system. Two of which are the Central Nervous System (CNS), and the Autonomic Nervous System (ANS). The Autonomic Nervous System has two branches; the Sympathetic Nervous System (SNS) and the Parasympathetic Nervous System (PNS).

The SNS drives the fight, flight, freeze response, while the PNS promotes rest and digest, also known as the rest and repair response.

The CNS is governed by your conscious mind, and you control it with your thoughts. For example, you decide to get up out of your chair and walk over to turn on the computer. You deicide it, you control your direction and pace. Your ANS however, is controlled by your subconscious mind. In other words, you are unable to access it with your thoughts. The ANS controls the functions of your body such as heart rate, cell renewal and digestion. You cannot suddenly wake up and tell the ANS to make you grow 3 inches taller, (believe me, I spent my teenage years trying and I'm still 5ft1 at the age of 42). It is the ANS that is so affected by a busy, hectic lifestyle and rushing. And you are enormously affected by the way your ANS responds.

It's possible that Melissa's stressful and busy life, lack of sleep and weight gain could indicate that her nervous system is being a challenge for her. If so, these are some of the symptoms which might be showing up in her body;

- Regularly feeling stressed or on high alert
- Inability to lose weight despite exercise and calorie counting
- Craving sugars and carbohydrates.

---

[2] Nutritional Biochemist Dr Libby Weaver (PhD)

- Reliance on caffeine or energy drinks.
- Uneasy sleep or waking up feeling still exhausted rather than rested and restored
- Failing to get to sleep by 10:00 PM, then getting a second wind and staying up until 1am.
- Feeling anxious easily.
- Breathing is shallow and quite fast.
- Finding it hard to say no, and feeling guilty when she does
- Finding it hard to ask for help

Seemingly unexplained weight gain, or a new-found inability to lose excess weight, is often a source of stress for women and adds further to their feelings of frustration at not being able to fit self-care and exercise into their hectic schedule. One of the most enormous health challenges of modern times is that the body can constantly be on the receiving end of fight or flight message. The branch of the nervous system that is activated by stress of any type is the Sympathetic Nervous System. It is the Sympathetic Nervous System that controls your 'fight, flight, freeze' response when your body perceives you are in danger. It gets you ready to run for your life! You breathe fast & shallow, your heart rate increases, you may sweat, (much like when you exercise intensely), and in addition to releasing adrenaline, your body releases cortisol into your bloodstream which triggers a flood of glucose to provide you with fast fuel to outrun the danger.

If you do then run for your life, you burn up this glucose, and once you're safely out of danger, your Parasympathetic Nervous System can start to do its work to slow your heart rate and your breathing, to move blood back to the digestive tract so you'll be able to digest food to stay well nourished, (you know that feeling of your tummy unknotting and relaxing after a time of great worry or anxiety? That's your Parasympathetic Nervous System helping you). Once your Parasympathetic Nervous System kicks in, your body feels 'safe' to burn fat as fuel, as a slow-release form of energy.

But we 21st century women seldom, well never, have to run for our life from a sabre-toothed predator. So, what happens when it's work, clients, meetings, emails, social media, marketing, money worries, growing children and aging parents that are making us stressed out each day? We feel overwhelmed, worry we're not a good enough Mum, wife, daughter, friend, and as a business owner,

One really simple thing you can do, anytime, anywhere to help activate your Parasympathetic Nervous System and calm your body is to *Take some slow breaths*. Try what I call 'Box and Belly Breathing'. Using your finger in the air in front of you, trace the four sides of a 'box' or square as you breathe in for 4, hold for 4, out for 4, hold for 4. If you feel you'd like to deepen further you can try in for 6, hold for 6, out for 6, hold for 6. As you do this, have your other hand placed lightly on your belly and feel your belly rise with your in-breath and fall with your out-breath. Long, slow breathing communicates to the body you are very safe and nothing downregulates the alarm signals within your body more powerfully.

Imposter Syndrome alert! We sometimes feel so inadequate we wonder when someone will 'find us out'! So we're carrying all this fear and stress, rush and overwhelm daily; our Sympathetic Nervous System is in overdrive, we've a knotted stomach, perhaps our heart rate feels high, we feel we're on red alert all the time. However,

unlike our ancient sisters' sabre-toothed predator, we cannot out run our overwhelming life tasks and priorities and the huge mental load we're carrying with us day and night.

If you push yourself hard enough, constantly, for long enough, you can end up in a state of Sympathetic Nervous System Dominance; so your body is constantly in fight, flight, freeze mode, constantly stressed and therefore rarely able to allow the Parasympathetic Nervous System to help you into rest and repair mode. You can feel totally overwhelmed with everything you have to fit into your day, guilty because you feel you're spread too thin, not able to give your best either at work, at home or in your significant relationships, you feel you're trying to do it all and end up doing none of it as well as you'd like. Add in coffee ("I need it to get going in the morning"), sugar ("I need the extra energy today"), high intensity exercise ("I need to burn off that chocolate right"), and alcohol ("thank goodness I can get my teeth unclenched a little at the end of the day") and you could be pushing your system further into Sympathetic Nervous System Dominance.[3] In this state, our Parasympathetic Nervous System rarely gets a chance to kick in and begin its valuable restorative work within our body and we can find ourselves in a state of chronic stress. Our long-term stress hormone is cortisol and for our ancient sisters, long-term stress always revolved around food scarcity. So, helpful hormone cortisol slows down your metabolism, meaning that you burn fat for energy more slowly; it's trying to help you survive this period of perceived famine but the effect for you is that no matter what you try you can't seem to shift that stubborn weight.

Perhaps this resonates with you. Many of the busy businesswomen I work with, like Melissa, feel this way when we first meet.

In the rest of this book, my purpose is to show you a clear 6 step method for exactly how you can stop the rush & overwhelm, to calm your body and mind and get back in control of your time, tasks & priorities. Once you've done that, many other aspects of life will fall into place for you. Are you ready?

I'd like to ask you to consider two questions:

[3]Nutritional Biochemist Dr. Libby Weaver (PhD)

- How is rush showing up in your life at the moment?
- How is busy-ness impacting you?

This rush, busy-ness and overwhelm won't just be effecting one area of your life. Take a look below at The Wheel of Life. How is the rush and overwhelm you're living with showing up in these eight different areas of your life? How is it effecting your significant relationships, your own self esteem, your time for personal and professional growth and development, your work or business life, your sleep, your health and wellbeing, your family time?

I'm going to ask you to rate where you are at the moment in your life. Using this wheel of life, give yourself a rating for each of the sections between zero and ten, zero being in the middle of the wheel and being the worst situation it could possibly be ten being the outside of the wheel and being the absolute best, most fulfilled and happy situation it could possibly be. Rate yourself between zero and ten in each section of the wheel and link up the dots with a line to see what kind of a shape you have. Don't worry if it's a wonky wheel! Most people have a wonky wheel when they first do this exercise.

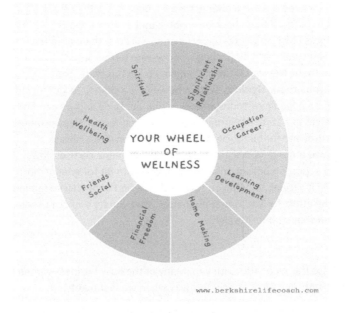

www.berkshirelifecoach.com

So how are you feeling about your wheel? It can be eye opening to take a really honest look at where you are in your life at the moment. Which of these areas are troubling you the most? In which of these areas are you tolerating things at the moment that you would love to change straight away? And can you notice how these different areas of your life interact with one another? The different parts of our life don't exist in silos, they're like a jigsaw. They all fit together to make the whole. This book takes an holistic approach. We're looking at you as the whole person, all the things that make

10

you who you are. Things that are causing you stress, rush, overwhelm or urgency at work or in your business will also be overspilling and having an impact on your important relationships or on your health and wellbeing or on your ability to sleep well. Equally, if you feel that you're struggling with the juggling at home, with family life, that will be having an impact on other areas of your life too; maybe it's causing you to feel you don't have the time or the wherewithal to look after yourself well, to do the exercise you want to do or to prepare and eat healthy food. Have a think, take stock. How are these different areas of your life bumping into one another, over spilling into one another and interacting and causing you discomfort and disharmony?

Next, I'd like you to think about where you'd like to be. Have another look at the wheel of life. Take one section at a time, and for each section ask yourself what would success look like and feel like for me in this area of my life? How do I want this area of my life to be? For each section make a real and detailed picture in your mind's eye about what you would like that area of your life to look like and feel like, sound like. Who else is there with you? What are you enjoying doing in that area of your life, and how is it making you feel?

Now we're going to look at the gap. You've looked at where you are in each section of the wheel. You've created a detailed picture in your mind's eye of where you'd like to be in each section of the wheel. Now let's try to quantify the gap. For some sections, for example, your health and wellbeing, you might be able to measure the gap in lbs. Perhaps you feel that you're overweight by your own standards and you have an ideal weight that you would like to reach; an ideal number of lbs that you would like to lose. Perhaps in your work or business section, you can measure it in £s. What does success in your business life mean to you? What are you turning over annually? What freedom is that income giving to you and your family? What does it enable you to do? Perhaps in other sections of the wheel you're measuring the gap by looking at the quality of a relationship, or the amount of time spent on a particular activity or with a particular person. There is always a way to measure the gap, you just have to get creative enough to find it.

Mindset change.
Before you read any further we need to address the thinking shift. I want you to wholeheartedly believe that there is another way to live life. To be a successful, happy and fulfilled woman in the 21st century, you do not have to accept that life is just this busy and overwhelming. There is another way. I'm going to show you that way in the rest of this book.

Homework. If you haven't done so already, do the exercises in this chapter. Actually get them down on paper. Doing them on paper is much more powerful than just doing them between your ears!

Booby traps to avoid

- You rush onto the next chapter without taking time to complete the exercises.
- You believe your life is different, you're the exception, this method won't apply to you.
- You don't really believe life can be less rushed and still be successful in all areas.

Keys to success

- Be honest with yourself about where you are now.
- Quantify the Gap.
- Believe life can be different.

**Chapter two. The second step; Purpose, Envisioning and Emotional Rocket Fuel.**

"We become so accustomed to the shape of our lives, that we think no other is possible.
Yet, of course, it is"

So, in chapter one you've taken stock, you've thought about your time and what living in a constant state of rush, hurry and overwhelm is doing to you and your important relationships. You've had a look at your wonky wheel of life and decided what you're currently tolerating in certain areas of your life that you'd love to change, you've looked at what you'd like to experience in that area of your life instead and you've quantified the gap.

Now may I ask you a question.

Why?

Why does it matter to you? Why is it so urgent and important that you change your relationship with your time and priorities? Your 'why it matters' will be tied up with what you feel is your 'purpose'.

> purpose
> *noun*
> 1. the reason for which something is done or created or for which something exists.
>
> "the purpose of the meeting is to appoint a trustee"
>
> 2. a person's sense of resolve or determination.
>
> "there was a new sense of purpose in her step as she set off"

In his work 'Man's Search for Meaning'[4] written in 1946, Austrian Psychotherapist Victor Frankel, wrote "The meaning of life differs from man to man from day to day, and from hour to hour. What matters, therefore is not the meaning of life in general, but rather the specific meaning of a person's life at a given moment. Everyone has his own specific vocation or mission in life to carry out a concrete assignment which demands fulfilment. Therein he cannot be replaced, nor can his life be repeated, because everyone's task is as unique as his specific opportunity to implement it."

From experience it seems to me that many of us, and I include myself in this, don't necessarily set before ourselves a specific 'purpose', or 'big why' in a strong way, until some sort of tragedy or near tragedy strikes us, for example nervous exhaustion, burn out, serious illness or loss. That's part of why so many busy women still, as I outlined in chapter one, continue to live each day without questioning the accepted wisdom that this is just the way 21st century life is.

Frankl urges us to "Live as if you're already living for the second time and you're about to act as wrongly as you did the first time round" and for many people, the decision to make a big change in the way they live their life, does indeed come after an experience such as a serious health scare, near death experience or a loss. As Nora McInerny remarks in her book 'The Hot Young Widows Club' "Imagine that moment when you slam on your brakes and stop just short of the bumper in front. That call you take where the bad news you never expected is delivered in a conversation that lasts just a few seconds. The birth of a child, everyone in the room waiting for that very first cry, the sound of life. The death of a loved one, the holy silence that follows that very last breath. These are moments that we do not rush to fill, that seem to quickly sort the chaos into manageable columns; that sort the real from the bullsh!t. They're only moments, quick visions of clarity before we're snapped back into the chaos. A moment of clarity I'd rather get without watching another loved one die".

Often, it is when we feel life has somehow 'given us a second chance' that it does suddenly matter to us, very much, to live a life based on our true priorities and purpose. Do you have a faith or a spiritual practise? Rely on it, lean on it.  At a time in my life when I realised I was completely not self-sufficient and needed gentle compassion. My personal spiritual practice is 'Thank God for Jesus' and this I do both formally, as part of the circle of compassion with other like minded humans, and informally throughout each day,

[4] Man's Search for Meaning Viktor Frankl

whether swimming in the sea, watching a sunset or waking in the middle of the night. Acknowledging a spiritual practice that connects us to something greater than ourself, often acts as emotional rocket fuel to keep us going when things get tough and keep us feeling purposeful, grounded and secure.

Steven Pressfield writes in his book The War of Art, "Have you heard this story; woman learns she has cancer, six months to live. Within days she quits her job, resumes the dream of writing Texmex songs she gave up to raise a family or starts studying classical Greek or moves to the inner city and devotes herself to tending babies with aids. Woman's friends think she's crazy, she herself has never been happier".

In his book 'Live it' celebrated performance coach Jairek Robbins tells how and why it suddenly became imperative to him to find and live out his purpose. It whilst living and volunteering in Kangulumira, a rural Ugandan farming village that Jairek became dangerously ill and was told he had only 5 days to live. He says "I was forced to confront in that moment the reality of my life. Not the someday goals or loose plans I had made, but how I had actually lived my life up to that point. The choices I had made, the priorities I had set, and what I had to show for myself. If I were to die in a few days, would I die feeling satisfied and content with my life, would I die knowing that I had lived a life that was truly worth living? Did I give back and make the difference that I was created to make?". He was 23 years old. Jairek was facing one of the most challenging moments of his life and as far as he could tell there were only a few options.

1. Give up, tap out and die
2. Cross his fingers and hope something good happened.
3. Find a reason to live and fight like hell.

Jairek spent the next few days digging for a purpose that he felt would make his life worth living. Up until that day, he had believed his purpose in life was coaching. He had helped hundreds of people make more money, lose weight, find fulfilling relationships, and achieve all kinds of other results. All of this was wonderful, but it lacked the depth he was searching for in the long run. When faced with his own impending death, he discovered that his ultimate goal and purpose in life was to inspire more people to focus on giving back and making a valuable difference in the world.

Digging deep and discovering your own purpose; why making this change matters to you, is essential because it will be the emotional rocket fuel you need to keep going when times get tough. If we don't identify our purpose, we tend to drift. We may still have a fulfilling, productive and fun life, achieving much and enjoying life, but, if you want to do hard things, if you want to make a change to the way you do life, if you want to truly discover another way of relating to time, priorities, to yourself and to other important people in your life, you're going to need some emotional rocket fuel to get you through the tough bits, through the parts when you feel like throwing in the towel and retuning to the safe familiarity of your comfort zone; to the way you've always done things. My passion and mission is to support busy women to question the accepted wisdom and implement a healthier way of living *before* a health scare, burnout or tragedy forces them to do so.

I'd like to tell you about Father and son team, Dick[5] and Ricky Hoyt[6]. A father who climbed mountains, ran marathons, travelled to the ends of the earth to give his son a better life; a life that transcended the limitations of his body, with their trademark motto. "Yes, you can!".

Marathons along with Ironmen are two of the toughest athletic endeavours on the planet, the ultimate test of strength and endurance. Team Hoyt are father son duo and what makes this duo so special is that the son was born with cerebral palsy and is quadriplegic and so his father Dick, pushes and pulls him in specialised wheelchairs, bikes and boats.

Richard Eugene Hoyt Junior was born January 10, 1962 in Holland, Massachusetts, the first son of Dick and Judy Hoyt. Dick says "The first time I saw Rick, he was in an incubator, and he was doing push ups and I said wow there my son he's going to be an athlete. He's doing push ups already and he's only two days old." Doctors told the devastated parents that their son would have minimal quality of life and recommended that he should be institutionalised. His parents were told to forget him, he is going to be nothing but a vegetable. "My wife and I, we cried and we talked about it and we said, no, we're not going to put Rick away like the doctor suggested, we're not going to put him in an institution, we're gonna bring him up just like any other child and this is what we have done."

In 1977 at age 15, Rick used his computer to ask his father if they could run together in a five mile road race to support a lacrosse player from his school who had recently been paralysed. Rick said "I wanted to show this person that life goes on and he could still live a productive life. That is why I turned to my Dad and said that we have to run in this race." Dick was 40 years old at the time and says "I was not a runner. I used to run, maybe, three times a week, a mile each time to keep my weight down. And all we had was a regular wheelchair prescription made for Rick and we had a hard time pushing him in it, never mind running with it, but we went down to the race. It was a five mile race, they gave Rick and I a number, the

---

[5] Dick Hoyt passed away 21st March 2021. Rick is still alive and competing in Boston Marathons.
[6] The story of Dick and Rick Hoyt

gun went off and Rick and I took off with all the other runners. Well, everyone thought that we would go to the corner and turn around and come back. We didn't; we finished the whole 5 miles coming in next the last but not last, and we have a picture of Rick coming across the finish line, he's got the biggest smile you saw in your life! When we get home that night Rick said on his computer "Dad when I'm running it feels like my disability disappears". Which was a very powerful message to me."

Team Hoyt knew they had to keep running. So they had a special racing wheelchair made for Rick, a streamlined three wheeler so they wouldn't keep veering off course. Team Hoyt steadily began doing longer and bigger races and eventually set their sights on the Boston Marathon race.

Organisers turned them down at first, but finally relented, although the Hoyts got no special treatment, they would only be allowed to participate if they qualified in Rick's age group. This was quite a challenge as Rick was in his 20s while Dick, the one who was doing the running was in his 40s, yet with determination and perseverance they qualified and so began a father and son legacy.

The Boston Marathon became an annual event for them, their personal record for The Boston Marathon is 30 minutes shy of the world record; a record set by an able bodied person running alone.

An Iron Man is arguably one of the world's most challenging one day sporting events. Initially begun as a contest in 1978 to see which athletes between runners, swimmers or cyclists were the most fit, the Ironman Triathlon has developed into a worldwide competition of determination. To say an Iron Man takes a lot of energy is an understatement. The average Iron Man competitor burns around 7,000 to 10,000 calories during those gruelling 226 km; that's 45 times the average daily intake. To most it would seem barely possible to do one by ourselves, but imagine how difficult, it would be to push and carry someone else. Well, that is exactly what Dick Hoyt did. For 226 kilometres he pulled, pushed and carried his son Rick.

Ricky says " A Triathlete probably weighs about 150lbs and their bike weighs about 17lbs. This is a total of 167 pounds. Dad weighs about 180 pounds and our bike weighs about 70 pounds because it needs to be heavier and stronger to hold both me and my seat. Dad isn't very pleased about this, but I now weigh about 100 pounds thanks in part to a regular diet of ice cream and chocolate cake."

The Hoyts have competed in more than 1,000 athletic events in the last 35 years. They ran the Boston Marathon 32 times, plus 39 other marathons and 252 triathlons, including six Iron man distance events. They ran across the United States of America through 18 states from Santa Monica Pier in Los Angeles to Boston Harbour,

Massachusetts. The whole thing distancing 6,011 kilometres and lasting 47 consecutive days, averaging 127 kilometres a day.

Why? What was Dick's purpose? "Dad when I'm running it feels like my disability disappears".

When your purpose has snapped clearly into focus and is so strong that it feels as if it would be impossible for you *not* to live it out, you can do anything! Do hard things with great love. You really can do anything you put your mind to, but you can't do it all at once, and just because you know what you need to do, doesn't mean you know how to go about doing it! You need a method.


A change of perspective; finding purpose in pain

One August evening as I was tucking my nine year old son into bed he asked "Daddy's illness isn't like Great Grandma's is it? He's not going to die?"
I replied "Oh no, you can't die of the type of illness Daddy's got. It's nearly September and that's nearly Christmas; we'll get Daddy better before Christmas, we can't have Christmas without Daddy can we!" I was so self-assured.

A month later, my husband, the boys' beautiful, gentle, loving Daddy, was dead.

As Levi Lusko wrote in his book 'Through the Eyes of a Lion', "Death doesn't always call ahead. It comes to us in a lot of ways, but often it is a surprise. 'Sir, you have six months to live' is not something anyone wants to hear, but if your doctor says that to you, know that it is a gift. Not just for you – because it forces you to confront your mortality and gives you the chance to prepare – but for everyone who loves you as well, because they will get the chance to say good bye." ..... ".. when death came to our home, it blindsided us. To say that we weren't expecting it is putting it mildly. It came out of nowhere and delivered a sucker punch so fast that we didn't have the chance to even think about flexing. Like a thunderous blow to the solar plexus, it knocked the wind out of us and left us gasping for breath on an emergency room floor."


I'm not going to tell you it was pretty in the aftermath of my husband's death, it wasn't. It was cold, dark and awful. I was clinging on by my fingernails and the last thing on my mind was being purposeful, empowered and productive. I was living for my children. Each day, they were what kept me going; I had to, absolutely *had* to be there for them and with them. I had to try to support them to come to terms with the loss of their beloved Dad; they were 6 and 9 years old at the time and they missed him painfully. Their emotional wellbeing, their growth, learning and nurturing their continuing zest for life became my absolute raison d'etre. Don't get me wrong, my kids had always been my number one priority, but now there was a new *urgency* about this, a new clarity with which I could see that they desperately needed me to provide them stability, to be emotionally available for them, not just outside of working hours before 8am and after 6pm, they needed me to be available to have the hard conversations and answer the difficult questions whenever they were ready to talk. They needed me to be the one who tucked them in each night, not for me to be away overnight at conferences and meetings. They needed me to be the one to help them into school each day and to hold them when their world was falling apart.

I'm a very visual thinker. At first, all I could see, all I could envisage, was that the traumatic loss of their Dad to suicide was going to negatively affect the entire rest of their lives. I was terrified. As C.S. Lewis wrote "Nobody told me that grief felt so like fear". I had to make some positive pictures with them. We made memories, we went places, we went on holiday, we painted and drew together, we had movie nights and board game afternoons (they were less willing participants in the board games but were usually persuaded). I began to take my lead from them; they were able to laugh. They were able to make new memories and they were able to learn new things and form new friendships and have fun! They still missed their Dad terribly, please don't think I mean that they were somehow suddenly past it or over it; far from it. But for the first time I could get a sense that life and love and learning was coming up around them and their grief, that while their grief may not be smaller, more and more positive, happy experiences were being added to their life and enveloping them. I could now, for the first time since my husband's death, see a picture of a happy future for our sons, with them laughing, playing and growing, emotionally secure and enjoying life. For us, many of these were by the sea and in my vision, the sea was always a part of our future happiness. I held that picture firmly in my mind. I took photos everywhere we went and made collages of happy memories. I thought "I have to nurture that. I have to do whatever it takes to enable that vision to happen. Their growth and wellness is my absolute number one priority, whatever that takes".

A year after their Dad's death, my older son moved from primary to secondary school. A big life event for a small boy; one he achingly wanted to share with his Dad.

Nearly three years after, my younger son received a diagnosis of Autism Spectrum Condition and Sensory Processing Differences. His mainstream primary teachers were absolutely brilliant with him and I will be forever grateful for their support and help, yet they and I agreed, his needs weren't being met in mainstream. He wasn't accessing learning, most days he couldn't even access the classroom, an echoey room in a Victorian building, chairs scraping on hard flooring, harsh, bright fluorescent lighting and 28 other children. It was an assault on his senses that he just couldn't cope with. During the summer of 2020, in the midst of covid and lockdown, we discovered that we lived only half a mile from a specialist setting appropriate for his needs. There were, at this time, only three of these particular schools in the UK that I know of and one was round the corner from our house! He was offered a place there and after a settling in period, it became apparent that it met his needs incredibly well and he began to flourish.

During this time, my older son was suffering. He hadn't taken well to secondary school life and adapted even less well to lockdown, becoming extremely anxious and isolated. His needs were entirely different from his younger brother's. There didn't seem to be a 'type' of school that would be a good fit for him and home learning certainly wasn't helping him. He needed a relaxed and accepting environment with a slower pace, preferably an outdoorsy place where he could access nature and animals. The only place I could find was 58 miles away and that just didn't seem doable.

His isolation and anxiety worsened over the months. His brother was settling into his new school and the change in him was inspiring to watch as he got the right interventions to help himself to regulate. It was incredible. Yet my heart was breaking for his older brother. One evening we ended up in A&E suspecting he'd broken his knuckles from punching his wardrobe door so hard out of grief and desperation.

I needed to act. I thought of my late husband and how much he would have loved and benefitted from a nature centred, outdoorsy relaxed school environment himself when he was young. I saw how down, deeply down, alone and anxious our firstborn son was. I thought of Dick Hoyt, and how for 226 kilometres he pulled, pushed, swam with and carried his son Rick. Over and over again, because "Dad when I'm running it feels like my disability disappears".

I knew I had to make some big changes; some mindset changes, some lifestyle changes.

I left my secure job of the past 15 years, where I had been very happy, and very busy. It had involved overnight stays for meetings and working long hours, commuting and then sometimes putting in extra time on the laptop in the evenings as well. I took a part time job closer to home that worked around the school runs and I enrolled myself at Performance Coach University, with a view to using my coaching experience, updating my training and starting my own business as a coach helping busy women and, I enrolled my older son at that school 58 miles away.

**Envisioning; a force for change**.

We're each of us different. Some people love envisioning and thinking in vivid pictures comes quite naturally to them. Other people may hear 'vision' or 'visualise' and think it's fluff; a nice chance to put together an attractive vision board or a rather self indulgent exercise in imagination. Those with a propensity to action, may feel very tempted to bypass this step of the method, but I promise you, it's essential! I hope this chapter has demonstrated to you how envisioning can be real and powerful agent for change; a tool that can get the human mind and body through difficult challenges and on to accomplish seemingly impossible achievements.

For those of you who are a mother, what got you through labour? Was it not (at least in part) the vision in your mind's eye of you holding your beautiful baby? Whether you realised it at the time or not, had you not had nine months of envisioning what it would be like to meet your child? What it felt like to hold them, to gaze into their tiny face? Had you not prepared the nursery, bought the tiny first outfits and mentally pictured your baby inside them? You had a vision of being a mother, a vision of meeting your baby.

What was it that kept you getting up to feed your newborn throughout the night? What was your purpose? Your purpose, a mother of a newborn, is no less than to keep your baby alive. In those early weeks they're completely and utterly dependent on you for their very survival. You know beyond shadow of a doubt why you're willingly and lovingly getting up 3 times a night despite your own body aching exhaustion; it's to feed your child to keep them or her alive. Nothing less.

Now, if at the age of 15 years they were still waking you every night at 1am, 3am and 5am to demand sustenance, I should think you might have a very different answer for them! Your driving force and purpose may still be to nurture and look after your 15 year old child, but by doing different things; they don't any longer rely on you for the same things as they did as a newborn.

We create things twice; first mentally, then physically. Vision is the first place where you engage your thinking about what is possible for you. The most powerful visions align your personal aspirations with your professional dreams. It's often your professional vision that funds and enables your personal vision. For your vision to help you push through the discomfort of change you must be clear on what it is you want to create in life. Don't just focus on your business, your business is just one part of your life and it's actually your life vision that gives relevance and meaning to your business vision.

Before you read further, we need to address the thinking shift.

Ask not how, but what if. How do we shift from impossible to possible thinking?

When we imagine a future that is significantly bigger than our current reality we can begin to think that it is impossible for us. The amygdala, the part of our brain that's designed to keep us safe, to avoid risk and uncertainty, kicks in when we experience uncertainty about how we can possibly create the future we are imagining. This part of our brain that avoids risk does a great job at keeping us safe in dangerous situations but when we start envisioning a bold future for ourselves, outside our current experience, the amygdala tries to shut the process down and keep us exactly where we are. The good news is that there's another part of our brain, the prefrontal cortex, which counter balances the amygdala. The prefrontal cortex lights up when you look out over sweeping beautiful views and open landscapes, and, when you imagine an exciting vision for yourself of your future. The capacity of our brains to change is called neuroplasticity, your brain has the ability to change and develop based on how you use it! The bad news is that unless you intentionally engage the prefrontal cortex, you are by default, relatively strengthening the part of your brain that keeps you stuck and resists change. You can strengthen your prefrontal cortex by regularly thinking about your compelling vision of your future. The neurons that fire in your brain when you think about your vision, are the same neurons that fire when you actually act on your vision. Isn't that amazing! You can train your brain to get more confident with your vision just by thinking about it!

We can take inspiration from others who have achieved great things, but we don't believe *we* can get there. Most people immediately ask themselves, "How would I do that?" However, this is premature. If you knew how to do it, you would be doing it already and living out your dream! The fact you don't know how to do it, creates the perception it's impossible, at least for you. As Henry Ford said "If you think you can or you think you can't, you're right". The first step to reaching your goal, is to shift from impossible thinking to possible thinking. You do this not by asking how, but by asking what if? What if you give yourself permission to entertain the possibility that you could make this vision a reality? What would be different in your life? If you were already standing in the results of this vision, what would be different for your family, for your friends, for your clients, for your community? Begin to allow yourself to connect with the benefits. By doing this, you'll probably find that your enthusiasm and desire to make this vision a reality intensifies. Maybe you can see now that your vision is a real possibility. Once you start to believe it is possible, you're now in a much stronger place to start planning *how* you might go about making this happen.

Another way of visioning.

There is another way to look at envisioning. This way is particularly useful if you feel you want to make a change in your life but something is blocking you, holding you back from taking that first step, from making that change. Perhaps you feel you're at a bit of a 'fork in the road' in your life and you're having trouble deciding which route to take, which decision to make. Will you Stick or Twist?

The Deathbed Vision.
Think about the decision or fork in the road you're struggling with at the moment. For example, let's say you're considering leaving the safety and familiarity of your current job to start up your own business. I'd like you to imagine you make a choice to leave work and start the business you love, right now, today.
Now imagine you're very elderly, you're on your deathbed, your time is up, right now, today, and you're looking back on your life. Maybe you'd like to imagine you're telling a grandchild or great grandchild about your life. Look back on your life as far back as this point today, to this decision to leave work and go self-employed. Imagine yourself describing to your great grandchild what life was life for you after that. Envision it in as much detail as you can. Hear yourself talking about it, are you happy, was it exciting, was it a fulfilling part of your life now you look back on it at the very end of your life?
Next, I'd like you bring yourself back to today. Imagine you make the other choice, take the other path. So, in our example, imagine you don't leave work and start up your own business. What does your life look like after that decision? Envision it in as much detail as you can. Hear yourself talking about it, are you happy, was it exciting, was it a fulfilling part of your life now you look back on it at the very end of your life?

While looking forward to a future vision builds anticipation, excitement and motivation, sometimes envisioning by looking back on your life from the very end of it can help you put things into perspective. As one client said to me "When I look back on it (their big decision) like that, the difficult bit that I'm worrying about seems smaller, less significant". It can also fill you with a determination not to reach the end of your life and feel it's been 'wasted', it can give you the urgency and impetus to take action toward achieving the life you actually want to live, the life you envisioned back in chapter two. As Dr Wayne Dyer said "Don't die with your music still in you".

In Melissa's email she's made it plain there are several areas of her life she's currently not happy in. I wonder what her ideal vision is for those areas of her life? If she had a way to manage her time and live a life led by her own top priorities, I wonder what that would look and feel like to her?

Action for the reader.

Identify your purpose; your big reason *why* managing your time better matters; what does it lead to? What does managing your priorities and schedule enable in your life, business and relationships? When you think you've identified this, ask yourself, "and what else?" Dig deeper, what else does managing your time and priorities lead to for you? What does it enable in your life? In your own wellness? What will it do for your important relationships? Lastly, when you've identified this, ask yourself "and what else?". Dig deeper one more time. What else does managing your time and priorities lead to for you? What does it do for your health? Your family? Your friends?

Make an absolutely compelling vision of your life that you connect to emotionally. Make it sensory, detailed with sights, smells, pictures, sounds. Write or draw or paint or collage something physical to hold your vision before you each day. Your vision should represent to you your purpose, your absolute reason for being.

Booby traps to avoid

- You have a bias straight to action and bypass the Vision exercise and move on. The problem is that when the going gets difficult, it's harder to stay committed to the work in the long run, because you have no compelling reason; no persuasive why.
- You create a 'token' vision that isn't personal and meaningful to you. Sometimes we are superficial in crafting our vision. We capture what we think we want or what we think we're supposed to want rather, than capturing what is meaningful to us. Keep coming back to it until you have something that you connect to emotionally.
- You don't connect your daily actions to your vision. Each day is a unique opportunity to either make progress toward your vision or to work hard to tread water. Take a few minutes to connect to your vision every day.

Keys to success

- Remember; our life vision informs and drives our business vision. Often our business vision finances our life vision.
- Make your vision as sensory and detailed as possible, make it vivid, clear and personal to you. Connect with it emotionally.
- Enlist peer support. Sharing your vision with others makes you feel more accountable to act on it.

## Chapter 3. Intentional Time Use.

**"The Key to juggling is to know that some of the balls you have in the air are made of plastic and some are made of glass"**

**- Norah Roberts**


"I just don't know where the time goes".

Have you ever caught yourself saying this? How often?

Many of us have experienced getting to the end of a day and finding that although we've been super busy working and rushing around all day, we haven't managed to cross off many of the tasks we had intended to do.  There are several reasons this tends to happen, here are some of the most common;

- You've found yourself frequently distracted and spent a lot of time reacting to things as and when they arise. For example, answering calls, messages and emails.
- You've procrastinated and put off tasks you know you needed to do.
- You've been jolted from your reverie by the postman at the door, only to realise you've spent the past 20 minutes down a social media rabbit warren.
- You try to Multitask.
- You can't say no, and now you've overcommitted.
- You read articles like this chapter all the time but never apply them.

Steven Pressfield from The War of Art: "Most of us have two lives; the life we live and the unlived life within us. Between the two stands Resistance. Have you ever brought home a treadmill and let it gather dust in the attic? Ever quit a diet, or course of Yoga? Late at night have you experienced a vision of the person you might become, the work you could accomplish, the realised being you were meant to be? Are you a writer who doesn't write? A painter who doesn't paint? An entrepreneur who never starts a venture? Then you know what resistance is.

Have you heard this story; woman learns she has cancer, six months to live. Within days she quits her job, resumes the dream of writing Texmex songs she gave up to raise a family or start studying classical Greek or moves to the inner city and devotes herself attending babies with aids. Woman's friends think she's crazy, she herself has never been happier. Is that what it takes? Do we have to stare death in the face to make us stand up and confront resistance?

Look into your own heart, unless I'm crazy, right now a still small voice is piping up telling you as it has 10,000 times the calling that is yours and yours alone. You know it, no one has to tell you and unless I'm crazy are no closer to taking action on it than you were yesterday or will be tomorrow".


Procrastination

If you tend to procrastinate, then you've probably asked yourself "Why? Why do I keep doing this?" Understanding why you procrastinate is a good starting point if you want to overcome it.

The main psychological mechanism behind our procrastination is as follows:

- When we need to get something done, we rely primarily on our willpower in order to bring ourselves to do it.

- Our willpower often receives support from our motivation, which helps us get things done in a timely manner.

- In some cases, we experience certain demotivating factors, such as anxiety or fear of failure, which have an opposite effect than our motivation.

- In addition, we sometimes experience certain hindering factors, such as exhaustion or outcomes that are far in the future, which interfere with our willpower and motivation.

- When demotivating and hindering factors outweigh willpower and motivation, we end up **procrastinating**, either indefinitely, or until we reach a point in time when the balance between them shifts in our favour.

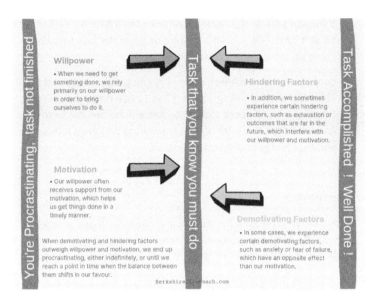

## Why do YOU do it?

As you read on, see which of these causes of procrastination resonate with you. Be reflective and honest with yourself while you do this; recognising the underlying causes of your procrastination is important if you want to spot it and successfully overcome it.

When it comes to specific reasons why people procrastinate, in terms of demotivating and hindering factors, the following are among the most common:

Abstract goals
People are more likely to procrastinate when their goals are vague or abstract, compared to when their goals are concrete and clearly defined. For example, goals such as "get fit" or "start exercising" are relatively vague and are therefore likely to lead to procrastination. However, a goal such as "go to the gym on Monday, Wednesday, and Friday straight after work, and spend at least 30 minutes on the treadmill, running at high speed" is concrete, and is therefore much more likely to lead you to take action. There are other things that can make a goal feel abstract. For example, if you've set a goal but you believe it is highly improbable you can actually achieve it, you will likely perceive this as an abstract goal, which in turn can increase the likelihood that you will procrastinate on it. More on this in Chapter Four!

Outcomes that are far in the future
People often procrastinate on tasks that are associated with outcomes (punishments or rewards) that they will

only experience quite a while after completing the task, because we tend to discount the value of outcomes that are far in the future. This is known as temporal discounting or delay discounting. For example, it's easier to discount the value of passing a test or an exam while that exam is still weeks away, compared to when it's only days away, which is one of the reasons why people wait until right before the deadline to complete necessary tasks (in this example, revising). People often display a present bias, this means they choose to engage in activities that reward them in the short-term, at the expense of working on tasks that would lead to better outcomes for them in the long term.

Prioritisation of short-term mood
Short-term mood repair, or hedonistic delay. People often procrastinate because they prioritise their feelings in the present and do things that will help them feel better in the moment, even if this comes at the expense of taking action that aligns with their long-term goals. Essentially, this form of procrastination occurs when people give in to their desire for instant gratification, and engage in behaviours that are satisfying in the short-term, instead of working on the tasks that will benefit them more in the long-term. This kind of behaviour relates to the tendency to seek out pleasurable activities and avoid unpleasant ones. While this tendency is natural and instinctive, it prevents us being at our best when we give in to it, as it causes us to continuously pursue short-term satisfaction, at the expense of long-term achievement and development.

A focus on future options
People sometimes avoid taking action in the present because they intend or hope to pursue a more attractive course of action in the future. This mindset can lead to long-term procrastination and persist even in cases where the person who is procrastinating never ends up following through on their intended plan. For example, a person might avoid starting to exercise on their own at home, because they plan to join a gym and start a detailed workout plan later, despite the fact that getting started now would still be beneficial and wouldn't prevent them from switching to a more serious exercise plan in the future.

Optimism
People who tend to be optimistic are often late. Frequently they're overly optimistic about how much they can get done in the time they have, try to pack too much in and end up late. Also, it can lead to them procrastinating on starting tasks as they think they'll easily have enough time to do it later or tomorrow. However, in some cases they underestimate the time it will take the to complete the tasks in question; (known as the planning fallacy), and it can lead

people to assume that they can complete upcoming tasks more quickly than they actually can.

Feeling overwhelmed
People sometimes procrastinate because they feel overwhelmed with regard to the tasks that they need to handle. A feeling of overwhelm can occur due to a having a single task that feels huge in terms of scope, or having a large number of small tasks that add up. When this happens, a person might simply decide to avoid the tasks in question, or they might attempt to handle them, but then end up feeling exhausted and paralysed before those tasks are completed.
For example, if you need to clean up your entire house, the fact that the task will take so long and involve so many parts might cause you to feel overwhelmed, in which case you might avoid getting started on it in the first place. More on this in Chapter Four!

Anxiety
People sometimes procrastinate because they feel anxious about a task that they need to handle.
For example, someone who feels anxious about checking their bills might repeatedly delay doing so, even though this avoidance won't make the problem go away.
This issue can be especially problematic in cases where a person's anxiety increases as a result of their procrastination, which can lead to a feedback loop where someone feels anxious about a certain task, which causes them to procrastinate instead of doing it, which makes them even more anxious, which in turn causes them to procrastinate even further.

Task aversion
I just don't want to.
People often procrastinate because they are averse to the tasks that they need to perform.
If you need to make an important phone call to someone you dislike, you might end up procrastinating instead of just getting it done, because you don't want to talk to them.

Perfectionism and / or fear of failure
Perfectionism or fear of failure can lead to procrastination in a number of ways, such as by making someone so afraid of making a mistake that they end up not getting started at all, or by making someone so worried about producing something with flaws that they end up reworking their project indefinitely instead of releasing it when it's ready. For example, someone might delay working on their book, because they want every line they write down to be perfect from, which causes them to not write anything at all. Similarly, someone who has finished writing their book might repeatedly delay sending it out for feedback, because they want to

make sure that it's absolutely flawless first, so they keep going over it, again and again. I will mention no names, (she says sheepishly, looking in the mirror).

Sensation seeking
People sometimes procrastinate because they like to wait until right before the deadline to start working on tasks, in order to add pressure, challenge, and excitement to those tasks.
For example, someone might wait until the night before a presentation is due to start working on it, because they feel that doing so will make the otherwise boring act of preparing the presentation more exciting. (Author raises hand).
In some cases, this type of delay can lead to positive outcomes, such as when it motivates a person to work hard on a task that they would otherwise find tedious. However, often, this sort of delay leads to negative outcomes in terms of performance.
Postponing tasks for this reason can often increase the amount of stress that people experience, and can also hinder their performance in situations where the delay means that they don't have enough time to deal with any unexpected issues that they encounter in their work or when they allow too many tasks to become last minute and are constantly working up against the wire.

Have you been reflective and honest with yourself while reading this?

Willpower has a fatigue factor.
As we've all experienced, sometimes we have the willpower and sometimes we don't. Leaving it up to willpower alone, you will likely find yourself procrastinating. In the rest of this book, I'm giving you the tools and support structures that make it easier to complete your planned actions than not to.

Michael Schumacher and Lewis Hamilton hold the record for the most World Drivers' Championships, both having won the title on seven occasions. Schumacher also holds the record for the most consecutive drivers' titles with five between 2000 and 2004 and Hamilton holds the record for the most race wins in Formula One history, with 103 wins to date. [7] I guarantee you, they had days when they didn't feel like getting in the car to practise or working out at the gym, but they did. That's because they have support structures in place that make it easier for them to get into the car / go to the gym than not to.

---

[7] Correct at time of writing

Here are some of the techniques to overcome procrastination which we will cover in the following chapters;
Prioritising
Establish a schedule/daily planner
Use time blocking
A deadline creates urgency
Practice self-compassion
Eliminate distractions
Overcome Imposter Syndrome
Manage your energy levels

**Let's start with Prioritising.**

**Steven Covey's quadrant.**
This is a useful tool to use at those times when you feel like there's so much to do a just not enough time to do it in all. You find yourself thinking, 'where does my time actually go?', the days are just rushing by and you seem to have been busy all the time but not achieved what you wanted to achieve. This is a great tool to help you find out where you're currently focusing, spending and investing your time, effort and energy; which quadrant are you spending time in? Where in your life and in your habits are you being productive and where are you finding that you're being not very productive at all?  This is also a good tool to help you prioritise what is actually urgent and important to you, because sometimes when we get busy and we feel overwhelmed, it feels as if we've been on the go the whole day without really achieving much. It's often because everything feels as if it's become urgent and important to us, as if there's no single ball that we can drop, nothing we can miss. This tool helps us to stop and take stock of what really is urgent or important to us in that moment. It's important to note that this is about what's important to *you*, there's no marking grid somewhere or correct answer about the things that are or are not important or urgent in life. What is important to you is going to be entirely unique to you and different from other people. It also depends what areas of your life you're using this to work on and where you are in your life at the moment. This is going to change; you could work with this when you were at college or university, you could work with it again when you're starting up your business or when your new parent or when you're planning a wedding, depending on when you're working with this, the things that you put in the urgent or important boxes are going to change as your time of life changes so please remember this is entirely personal to you. There's no right or wrong answer, this is about where you are, at the moment, in your life and with your family and relationships so you need to be bravely honest with yourself when you're filling this in. Let's have a look at Coveys Quadrants.

| MANAGE | FOCUS |
|---|---|
| CRISES AND PRESSING PROBLEMS | ON STRATEGIES AND VALUES |
| DEMAND + NECESSITY | OPPORTUNITY + PLANNING |
| DAILY FIRE-FIGHTING | KEEP CRITICAL THINKING |
| BE QUICK TO DELEGATE | CONSIDER THE MACRO |
| IMPORTANT/URGENT | IMPORTANT/NOT URGENT |
| AVOID | LIMIT |
| INTERRUPTIONS AND BUSY WORK | THE TRIVIAL AND WASTEFUL |
| ILLUSION + DECEPTION | ESCAPE + WASTE |
| NOT YOUR EMERGENCY | ENTERTAINMENT ONLY |
| MINIMISE INVESTMENT | USE TO MINIMISE STRESS |
| URGENT/NOT IMPORTANT | NOT IMPORTANT/NOT URGENT |

When we're talking here about something important, we're meaning something crucial to you, something meaningful to you, something valuable, something you've deemed important in your value system in your life. When we're talking about urgent, we're talking about something time bound, it has to be done now, there's a time pressure, it can't wait, it can't wait till tomorrow, it can't wait till next week, it has to be done now.

Let's start looking in the top left quadrant. This is firefighting. Things that you would put into this quadrant are when you find yourself putting out fires, when you find yourself dealing with what feels like constant crises, things that are necessary and need doing now, need doing in a hurry, these are pressing problems or deadlines that you find yourself up against. Some people depending on your personality type, like working up against a deadline, (sensation-seeking procrastination, remember?) For some people, that time pressure makes them feel as if they're more energised and focused on their work, but for this quadrant you need to manage what you allow to go in there. If you allow too much to be right up to the wire, right up against that deadline, you're allowing no contingency time, no time for things that might go wrong if that deadline really isn't flexible. Being frequently in this quadrant is often what makes you feel like you're just always in a hurry and that your to do list is never ending, because as soon as you knock a few jobs off the top of it more stuff has come into this urgent space because it was stuff that needed looking at a week ago or two weeks ago and if you didn't get to it, the last minute stuff is constantly queuing, backlogging and coming into this quadrant. So, you can see that you really do need to manage what you allow to become urgent, what you don't deal with earlier, what you allow into this quadrant.

You also need to manage the stuff in this quadrant so if there are some real crises and pressing problems, which there will be from time to time, you need to decide how you're going to manage those. For example, some of those crises or pressing problems that arise, are you able to delegate, are you able to ask somebody else to deal with it or to do it? You also just want to check in with yourself when you thinking you're putting something into this quadrant, has it actually become urgent and important to you, or is it somebody else's problem? Is it somebody else's urgent that you're mistakenly putting into your quadrant one? You'll see in a minute where you might actually better place that if it's somebody else's emergency or urgency but it's not urgent to you at that time. So, manage what you allow to become urgent. When you do have pressing problems or crises how can you manage those? You can manage them by allowing for some white space in your diary, some contingency time, because emergencies will genuinely arise now and then. We're trying to keep you out of this daily firefighting quadrant as much as possible.


Let's look now across to quadrant 2 which is the top right-hand corner on the graphic where it says Focus. This is a highly productive quadrant for you to be spending your time in. This is a place where you feel peaceful and happy because you're ahead of the curve, this is where you can work on things that you truly value, you can perhaps do your planning, this is where opportunities unfold and you've got the space for critical thinking and creativity and this is the quadrant where you're taking into consideration your macro goals, your bigger vision and you're considering how what you're doing here is feeding in to those goals. When you're wanting to be productive and work towards goals, you're trying to attain this quadrant two is a really great place to be. An example of this kind of thing might be if you know you've got a test or exam you've got to study for and it's important but it's not yet urgent. That exam isn't tomorrow, that exam is still two months away, so you've got two months to study, to test, to strategise how you're going to study for that exam, it's not yet become urgent. Whereas if you leave it to the night before the exam that task has then moved straight across to quadrant one, it's become important and urgent because it's now the night before the exam, you want to try and keep that kind of task in quadrant two by doing that with still some time out, some time before that deadline. Get the bulk of that work done so that you're ahead of the curve and I say again, these things in quadrant two, are the things that you know *you* value, this is about you personally, so when you're filling this in for yourself don't be thinking this is the sort of thing that *should* be in here or *ought* to be in here; it's about you and what you're working on, the goals you want to move towards and the things that you value doing in your life, that's the kind of thing that needs to be in your focused quadrant here in quadrant two. That's not just about work and business, that's about your family, that's about your self-care time, your own wellbeing. For example, I make sure I absolutely plan into my focused productive quadrant two time my wellbeing time, be that my bath or my yoga or my going for a walk or my time with the children. Quadrant two is all about what is valuable personally to you, that you want to focus on, that feeds into your goals that you've set yourself in all those areas of life we looked at back in Chapter One, on your wheel of life. It is the work you do here in quadrant two which you're going to find is moving you closer towards achieving those goals.

Quadrant three, if we go down and to the left-hand side the quadrant where it says 'avoid'. These are often somebody else's emergency not your emergency, so these things sometimes you mistakenly put them into quadrant one, into the firefighting, demand, necessity. Just check in with yourself because sometimes they are not, sometimes they are somebody else's urgency not yours. For example, if you're busy working in quadrant two, you're focused, you're planning, you're achieving your plan for the day and then you suddenly get a phone call out of the blue that's trying to put you into quadrant three, part staying out of quadrant three is being fair and firm about your boundaries. Setting boundaries, being able to say actually "I can't do that right now" or " I can't have that conversation right now". It's when, for example, someone phones up and just starts talking at you and you can tell they want to tell you everything they've had since breakfast and you're going to be on the phone for 30 minutes, it's feeling comfortable to say "I'm sorry, I'm in the middle of something at the moment, can I call you back later?" When we learn boundaries and when we learn assertiveness we can start moving things that would otherwise be taking up our time in quadrant three and moving them into quadrant two, because if you're planning for it, if it's something you want to do, if it's a friend you want to speak to, you're not saying "no go away I don't want to speak to you", instead you can move it to a time when you've planned for it and you've allowed time for it and when you're going to really enjoy that conversation rather than being caught on the hop picking up the phone when you were in the middle of doing something else. That person is trying to make their urge to talk to you right now this minute into your emergency and it isn't, so if it's an interruption or not your emergency you can reframe it and move it into quadrant two and do it at a time when you want to do it, you've planned to do it and you know that you're going to enjoy it and get some benefit out of it rather than allowing it to be an interruption. The other thing that often ends up here in quadrant three is busywork, things that we know we don't really need to be doing right now but perhaps we're trying to distract from something we'd really rather not do. Let's go back to that example of studying for an exam, maybe now in quadrant three you know you should be studying for that exam coming up and suddenly, as if by magic you have the overwhelming urge to clean your kitchen instead. You know it doesn't need doing right now, cleaning the kitchen at that moment is not urgent or important right in this moment but you're trying to avoid something that perhaps you don't feel like doing. As you go through your week and use this tool, be honest with yourself about when you're putting yourself in quadrant three with some busywork.

Quadrant four, things that you consider not urgent and not important. Again, I really want to stress that this is about *you*, your value system, your life so whatever it is you consider important that's important on this grid, the things that you want to limit in quadrant four, things that you yourself don't consider to be important, don't consider to be urgent. You want to stay out of quadrant four. Sometimes this is stuff that we end up just doing on autopilot without really thinking about it and then we turn around and wonder where the past 15 minutes has actually gone because we just lost focus and drifted away. Like when we just end up scrolling, scrolling, scrolling aimlessly on social media or you hit a link which takes you to another link, which takes you to another link and before you know it, you think "how did I end up here?" You have gone right down that rabbit hole of following story after story link after link and you don't know where you've ended up and suddenly 20 minutes have gone out of your day, and you really didn't intend to spend this way. It's different if it is intentional, for a reason, if you were researching something on social media that's different but I mean the times when suddenly you sort of wake up after you've just been on autopilot in a bit of a daze thinking "where did the last 15 minutes go?" that's the kind of thing that you want to limit or minimise; things that you consider to be a bit trivial or a bit wasteful of your own time. I stress again this is not the quadrant to have things like self-care in. Your self-care is important, your self-care goes under wellbeing and that should be in quadrant two, you focus on things that make you feel good, things that make you feel filled and fuelled. This quadrant four is about the things that you deem to be not important and not urgent.

How to use it.
Use this sheet, this graphic, carry it around with you and for the next 3 days or so, whatever happens throughout your day, whatever you're doing, I just want you to make a note, jot it down in one of those four quadrants. Be honest with yourself when you have that conversation or when the phone rings or when your mother-in-law ask something of you when you need to go to the supermarket shopping, or your child suddenly need you for something put it in one of those quadrants where you consider it to be.

1. Is it something that you need to manage? Is it's urgent and important and it needs doing now, but ask yourself does it need to be done by you? Is it something someone else can do?

2. Is it a focused task that you want to be doing that's moving you towards your goals?
3. Is it something that you want to avoid for that moment? Is it a distraction or someone else's emergency? Do you need to say, "I can't do this right now I'm in the middle of something, but I can do this later"?
4. Or is it something that you want to limit for yourself because you think it isn't important and it isn't urgent.

Write it down, write it all down, the big things, the little things, the silly things, everything just so it's there and then sit and take stock. Have a look at where you have ended up spending lots of your time. Ask yourself, are you happy with the way this quadrant is looking? Are you happy with where you're spending your time? Do you feel you've been productive and focused? Have there been a lot of fires that needed fighting and what happened? Were you able to delegate them? Where can you improve? Where can you move yourself out of some quadrant one, three or four activities to give yourself some more time in quadrant two? Sometimes it might be that it opens your eyes to a bit more work that you want to do; so if you do find that you're spending a lot of time in quadrant three because you're making other people's emergencies your emergency, if you're saying yes to everything and letting other people make you feel that it needs doing right now, that might be telling you that perhaps you want to do a bit of work on your personal boundaries. This is not at all unusual and we're going to look at the importance of Yes, No and Not Now next in this chapter.

**The importance of Yes, No and Not Now.**

In order to be able to set some healthy boundaries and to be able to say no or not now we need to align our thinking with the core belief that it is OK to say no. From an early age many of us have a blueprint that it is not OK to say no when people ask us to do something or to be involved in something. In the moment it can be hard to say no because we don't want to disappoint anyone. There's someone standing right there in front of us, and we have the opportunity to contribute and to help them out, it feels so much better to say yes than to say no but while saying no may disappoint them in the moment it is much better in the long run than overcommitting yourself and then not delivering on your promises. I know that most people would rather hear you say no than say yes and then let them down at the last minute or not be able to deliver what you committed to. When you say yes to something take your word seriously, value your word, if you said yes to something value keeping that commitment and avoid making promises you know you cannot or will not keep. Don't take on more than you can handle. When you say no or not now to somebody you're actually doing them a favour, it may not feel like it in that moment but you're setting their expectations, they know where they stand with you and you're doing yourself a favour too because by explaining that you just can't get involved with what they're asking of you at that time they know what to expect, you've already made your decision and you've got that off your mind. Whereas, if you say yes to something you know you really haven't got the time for, that's going to be playing on your mind as you try to keep that commitment which you know you don't have the time to keep. Often, we try to avoid short term relationship pain by saying yes when we know we should say no. The problem is that when we break our word, we potentially damage that relationship and maybe others feel they can no longer rely on us. It can be difficult to learn how to say no or not now. If we are serious about changing our relationship with time and serious about committing to those actions that are going to bring us closer to achieving our goals and living the life we envisioned back in Chapter two, we're going to have to learn what to say yes to and how to say no to the things that don't align with the vision of our life.

Sometimes we find it hard to say no because we're carrying around a mistaken belief that saying no is somehow bad or rude. This can be deeply ingrained in us and can go right back to early childhood when we were encouraged to be compliant and to say yes rather than refusing things. We sometimes say yes when we don't want to because we are worried or concerned about the other persons reaction, we don't want to hurt, offend or upset them. When you're put on the spot and asked to do something or get involved with something or commit to something it's easy to find our mouth saying, "yes sure I can do that for you" whilst our brain is saying "no, no, what you are saying, be quiet". Saying yes seems to trip naturally off the tongue for some people, I should know I'm one of these people. It can be incredibly helpful to have some stock phrases, things that you feel comfortable with tucked in your hat for these occasions where you feel you've been put on the spot. Something that manages the other persons expectations fairly, that is positive and uplifting but doesn't lead them on to thinking that you may be going to say yes when you know that you can't do it. Hold it in your mind that saying no doesn't just help you, it helps the other party as well. It helps you manage your time and priorities, it helps them manage their expectations and know where they stand. It also helps other people to see you as reliable. If they know that you know your own mind and can say no then they know they can rely on you, that if you say yes you'll be able to carry that through and keep your word. This integrity helps both your personal and professional reputation. You will likely find that the vast majority of people accept your no or not now graciously and without difficulty. However, we all know someone don't we, who knows just how to make us feel guilty for saying no. At some point, this will happen. Don't allow it to set you back, let's be ready for it. When you use your politely declining phrase with a smile and the other party tells you, (or someone else) how jolly self-centred they think you've become, emotional reasoning will do a number on you. It goes like this; "I knew it was rude to say no. I've said no and now this person is cross and they're saying I'm rude, I feel guilty so they must be right, I must have something to feel guilty for; I *am* rude!" And before you know it you're apologising for being so thoughtless and changing your no to a yes, leaving you frazzled, once again overcommitted, time strapped and now feeling guilty and insecure to boot. Allow people their reactions. You can control your yes, no or not now. You cannot control their reaction to it. And, you don't know what might happen for them further down the line; you may see their initial annoyance and surprise as the girl who just can't say no, says no to them, and seems comfortable to do so, but what ripple effect may it have later? Many, many people I know struggle with being over committed because they struggle with saying no. What if you start a revolution? What if they go off and ponder at your new found ways, get over their initial anger and try out politely declining for themselves too? Don't fall at your first hurdle, get up, dust yourself off and keep intentionally deciding how you want to spend your time; what you'll say yes to, what you'll say no to and when you'll say not now thanks.


Action for the Reader:

Spend some time now trying out ways to politely decline. Practise saying no! Right now. Say some different phrases out loud, test them out, see how they feel. At first, they'll likely all feel hideously uncomfortable and you'll feel the urge to take it back and say yes, because that's what you've spent years training your brain to do! Stick with this. Keep digging deeper, you can do this. Find a phrase to decline a social invitation and a different one for a work related project. Now also test out ways to tell someone you're not sure and would like to think about it and get back to them. Keep practising these out loud to yourself in front of the mirror. Your brain, your ears and your mouth, have experienced years of feeling and hearing you say yes, yes, yes. You've programmed yourself this; you've made this your default setting through repetition. You need to give your brain, your ears and your mouth many experiences now of feeling and hearing you saying your declining phrases. You need to become comfortable with using them. The more you say them to actual real people and discover the world doesn't end and you don't end up a social pareira as a result, the more you'll begin to feel it's ok to say no or not now.

Keys to success

- Practise out loud in front of the mirror, not just inside your head.
- Practise regularly. If you're going to a meeting, function or event where you think you might need this, have an extra practise just before going.
- Remind yourself that most people would rather hear you say no, than say yes and then let them down at the last minute and not be able to deliver what you committed to.

Booby traps to avoid

- You think that thinking these inside your head will do just as well. It won't. Say them out loud.
- The first time someone reacts badly to you saying no, you feel guilty and change your no to a yes. Don't do it!

**Reactive time and focused time. Control Interruptions and distractions**

**"During these kind of days I always think, with merriment, about the legendary story of Samuel Taylor Coleridge beginning to write Kubla Khan in a fever dream before being interrupted by a person from Porlock and then becoming furious at losing his vision forever. I think it's repeatedly mentioned as one of the all-time stories of frustrated literary ambition because it's the only instance in history where a man was interrupted whilst doing some work. Women have 15 'persons from Porlock' a day." - Caitlin Moran**

Many of the tasks that derail us during the day and take us away from our intended work are reactive tasks; with emails, texts and social media notifications it's quite possible that our laptop and our phone are buzzing, ringing and beeping throughout the day, constantly interrupting our flow and our train of thought and our deep work. Part of the method is to separate your focused time from your reactive time. Depending on your role and what you're working on you may need different amounts of reactive time to do the administrative tasks and reply to the emails, messages and phone calls; for some of you one block of 30 minutes a day might be enough, others of you may need two blocks of 30 minutes or three blocks of 30 minutes. Don't put in more than three reactive blocks a day. When scheduling some reactive time into your daily plan, for many of people it works well to have one reactive block at the beginning of the day and one reactive block at the end of the day. If your role involves a lot of administration and replying to emails, phone calls and messages you may want to add a third block in the middle of the day. These reactive blocks are the times you are going to commit to replying to those emails, messages and notifications; outside of those blocks turn off the notifications.

Yes.

Really.

Turn. Them. Off.

Take back control of those distractions.

Don't allow the buzzing, binging, ringing to distract you, turn off the email notifications, turn off the social media notifications and stick to reacting to incoming messages during your reactive blocks. Some of the busy women I work with have found that it's really helped them to also add a note to their auto responder that says, "I check and reply to my messages at these times of day you may not get a response outside of these times", it helps manage their colleagues' and clients' expectations. Implementing this has helped so many of my clients feel much more in control of their time and be much more productive because they're not getting constantly derailed by reacting to other things. It allows you to be productive and focused and get through the deeper work that you want to concentrate on, the strategic work that moves you further toward your goals. If the worry or concern is that your clients or colleagues on the other end are waiting for your response, put on your auto responder message. This manages their expectations and lets them know that they will hear from you and tells them when they will hear from you, it also lets them know that you're organised and that your time is valuable, that you're busy because you're good at what you do and your work is in demand, that you have received their message and that they will get a response from you at a certain time. It's important you do therefore respond during your reactive time so that they know they can trust this and rely on you to do so. If it's a complicated response that is needed which would involve a bigger piece of work or more research, during your reactive time reply with a holding email just letting them know that you have received their message and that you're working on it and will get back to them when you have a fuller answer.

The times between your reactive blocks are your focused times, your replenishment times and times for doing the other important day to day tasks, such as client appointments, networking, exercise, the school run, meal prep time and eating times, family time, social time and sleep.

Focused time.

Think back to your quadrant two activities, whether these are work related, family related, health and wellbeing related, these are your planned in, scheduled actions, things you've intentionally chosen to focus on. In Chapter four you will identify some Winning Action Commitments, things that you identify will move you towards your vision of the life you want to live. These Focused time blocks are going to be filled up with your Winning Action Commitments.

As well as your Reactive time and your Focussed Time there will be other day to day necessities such as your sleep time, your personal care time, commuting or travelling time, client appointments, networking meetings, the school runs, meal times, exercise and the other things you need to fit in to your days. Can you see how when you use your schedule as a planner you start building it up like a jigsaw? The picture may look and feel rather full at first, but when you look at it you will see that all the important and essential activities that you want and choose to prioritise in your life are covered by using this method. It's essential to get your schedule down in writing, whether that's in a paper planner such as comes free with The Method course or an electronic calendar if that's your preference, as long as whatever you use has an hour by hour breakdown of the days. If you can't make your day to day schedule work on paper, there's no way you're going to make it work in practice.

Keys to success

- Outside of your reactive blocks, turn off ALL notifications, even the small icon that silently appears to tell you 'you've got mail' will be a visual distraction and send your brain wondering about what that tantalising unexplored new message may contain.
- Allow yourself enough reactive time, just make sure you stick to 'blocks' and don't let it encroach
- Value your focussed time, treat it as important, protect it. Keep those appointments with yourself.

Booby traps to avoid

- You just cannot bring yourself to turn off notifications, so you keep them on and think you'll be able to ignore them. You won't.
- When life gets busy, you allow your focussed blocks to get squeezed out by other demands on your time. This way, you'll still not get the stuff done that's important to you.

So, what do we do when our day to day schedule doesn't work on paper?

**Outsourcing: what it is and why do it.**

If there are more tasks in your life and in your business then you can comfortably fit into your schedule on paper then you are never going to comfortably fit them in in reality. We've looked at what's urgent, what's important and what's unnecessary; what about the stuff that is important and needs doing but doesn't necessarily have to be done by you? I've seen this come up often with women I work with who are business owners when their business is maturing and has been around a while. Usually they started out as a sole trader and everything in the business fell to them but now their business has grown and in some ways they're feeling a bit like a victim of their own success. Often at the point a client comes and starts working with me they're saying "I left my corporate job because I wanted to start my own business doing something I love doing in a way that would fit around my family and my other life commitments but now I'm finding I'm working longer and harder than I've ever worked in my life!" They're not feeling the freedom of time they had anticipated when they left their corporate job to start their own business. Your own business is usually something you care very passionately about, it matters to you how it's done and the idea of somebody other than you doing important tasks in your business can be quite difficult at first to come to terms with and that's okay. This next section is going to gently talk through how we can make this journey successful for you.

If you're a mum, do you remember the first time you left your baby with someone else? I do, vividly, both times. With my first son he was two months old and I left him home with my husband while I went to town all on my own for two hours shopping! With my second born he was four months old and I left him with my mum for about 3 hours while I was at a PTA meeting at my elder son's pre-school. Each time felt like a hugely big deal to me, each time it mattered immensely to me who I'd left my precious baby with and how they'd look after them. Well, you also love your business; you've worked so hard building your business, you value your clients, you like the way you do things, it matters hugely to you that when you outsource a part of that, you're giving that responsibility to someone you trust, someone you know will serve your clients and the good name of your business well.

So, are you doing more of what you love? Or are you busier than you've ever been before chasing invoices, booking appointments, promoting and marketing your business, seeking out potential new clients, doing your accounting and admin, oh, and squeezing in some of what you love doing too? I mean, that's why you started your business right? That's your genius zone, your golden time, what you are really excellent at, what lights a spark within you. When we first start out it's natural that we're the ones doing just about everything in our new business but as it grows and grows it's going to reach a point where you're faced with a choice; keep trying to do it all yourself but you're already at the limit of your own capacity so growth will stall, or start to outsource some parts so you can concentrate on doing what you're really excellent at and so you can continue to scale and grow your business. Makes sense? Despite the sense it makes it's understandable that you will at first find it very difficult to do. Here are some things to think about on this journey.

- Outsourcing is a great way to continue to have capacity to grow your business.
- It gives you more time to do what you're best at thus driving your business forward.
- There's no rush; network, get to know a few people who do the thing you're looking to outsource, look at their current work if you can, do a bit of research, ask for recommendations from people you trust.
- Take a suck-it-and-see approach at first rather than tying yourself, and them, into a long contract.
- Have honest conversations about what exactly you're looking for from them and ask whether that's something they can deliver or not.
- Make some standard operating procedures for them so they know not just what tasks you want them to do, but also *how* you want those tasks completed.

Chapter four

**Smart Goal setting, Winning Action Commitments & Costs and Scheduling.  ECOC.**

"Tell me, what is it you plan to do,
With your one wild and precious life?"
- Mary Oliver from her poem The Summer Day[8]


Hi Ellen,

I wanted to let you know, I have definitely seen some improvement but I'm struggling!

I've looked at my (very) wonky wheel of life and identified the areas I really want to change. I've thought about where I want to be and how to measure the gap, and oh my goodness , Covey's Quadrant! What an eye opener; I think I just live in Quadrant One almost all of the time! I can see now that part of the reason is I do overcommit, so I am trying to be brave and say no to some things and that is actually helping. I know it's also because lots of stuff seems to crop up at the last minute and I don't feel I have enough time to respond, or rather, because I try to make sure I respond, I'm then not doing other stuff I want and need to do. I've decided, for my own wellbeing and feeling better I'm going to lose 20lbs, and make sure I get more sleep. For the business, I'm going to increase turnover by 25% between now and April. I'm going to definitely spend more time with the children after school and on weekends and make sure we all eat more healthy, homecooked meals together (which will help with my weight loss too. Bonus!). Oh, and I joined my local fitness in the park group, but haven't managed to go yet, but I will.

The thing is, I feel I'm busier than ever! I'm chasing my tail all the time and although I feel I want to do these things, I don't seem to be actually making progress, which is really getting me down. We are off to the coast next week though, which I really need.

I just wondered, have you suggestions of what might help please?

Melissa

---

[8] Mary Oliver from her poem The Summer Day

In Melissa's message above, she has told us all the things that she's identified that she wants to change, but she hasn't told us how she's going to go about it. It's no wonder she feels busier than ever and as if she's chasing her tail! Planning is essential. Planning enables you to allocate your time and resources to your highest impact actions and this increases your odds of successfully achieving your goals. However, in spite of the many proven benefits of working from a plan, many people don't do it. One reason for this is that lots of people have a bias for taking action, and while an action bias can be a good thing, it can get you started and action creates momentum, it can also get in the way of you effectively making progress towards your goals.

Thinking shift. Before you read any further we need to address the fact that an effective plan takes an investment of your time to create and requires some hard work. It may seem counter intuitive but taking time to plan upfront can significantly reduce the overall time and effort to complete a task, and it can significantly increase the progress you make through your actions. In other words, if you plan to take the right actions, (the high impact actions, the Winning Action Commitments), you will find you're less busy, yet making greater progress towards your goals. Another reason that some people don't work from a plan is that they have a belief that as they already know what to do, they don't need a plan to get it done. Unfortunately, there is almost always a gap between what people know and what they do. Many of us want to get into better physical shape and virtually all of us know what that takes, but unfortunately many of us don't ever lose the weight or become more fit. That's because simply knowing what to do isn't enough. The world is noisy. The unexpected happens, distractions arise. As Iain Thomas wrote "Every day, the world will drag you by the hand, yelling, 'This is important! And this is important! And this is important! You need to worry about this! And this! And this!' And each day, it's up to you to yank your hand back, put it on your heart and say, 'No. This is what's important.'"

Our natural desire to stay in our comfort zone tugs at us and we lose focus on the things that we intended to do. This is why to successfully get more done in less time, make progress while being less busy and free up your precious time one of the most powerful things you can do is to create and work from a written plan.

**Do what you're doing while you're doing it.**
One thing at a time.

Like Melissa, I know many of you are juggling lots of different goals in different areas of your life and business and feeling quite overwhelmed. A research study by Amy Dalton and Stephen Spiller found that the benefits of planning diminish rapidly if not altogether if you pursue and plan too many goals at once. The study suggests that the act of planning for multiple goals itself discouraged people when they were forced to consider all of the obstacles and the costs involved in reaching their goals.

Remember previously, we mentioned procrastinating because a task seems too big and overwhelming? For example, if you are confronted with a big project such as cleaning a very messy house with multiple rooms plus many sub projects such as piled high laundry and dirty carpets, you can feel overwhelmed and fail to take any action at all.

When you start writing a plan that identifies the costs that must be paid to reach the goal, you think about the magnitude of the effort involved, and this affects your willingness to take any action. Imagine for a moment that you're trying to do all the things Melissa is trying to do. She's decided she's going to lose 20 lbs, sleep better, increase the turnover of her business by 25%, spend more time with her children and start a regime of home cooking meals herself. Now imagine you add one more thing to that list. For example, she's driving from London to the coast for a holiday. On top of everything else on your plate, you've just added a new goal (family holiday) and a new plan, (the directions to drive there). According to the research, you should now be feeling overwhelmed and rejecting plans altogether, making decisions based on what feels right to you in the moment instead. That is the place some people get to; have you been there? Have you ever cancelled plans because you just felt that you couldn't show up and carry out one more thing, you just wanted to hide on the sofa under a blanket because that felt good in the moment? I expect we've all been there at one time in our lives, I know I have!

However, often we do push through and get in the car and using the directions, arrive at the destination. So how is that possible? Well, you are only actually taking one action at a time while you are driving. You are not cooking home cooked meals or exercising, losing weight or increasing your business turnover while you drive. You focus instead on your directions, one turn at a time, until you reach your destination. Therefore, you're not thinking about the trip in a way that overwhelms you. Using that trip approach works with your other goals as well. The drive confines your focus because you physically cannot do anything else while you drive, all you are doing is focusing on driving. The Dalton and Spiller study also confirms this. It found that if you *think* your plan to reach multiple goals is manageable, then you are more likely to complete it and planning becomes beneficial for multiple goals as well. In other words, the way you think about your plan affects your ability to carry out your plan. There are ways to change our thinking about the goals that we're trying to achieve, ways to break them down into smaller, manageable tasks. Melissa is trying to pursue several goals at one time. She needs to shrink the magnitude of this challenge in her mind's eye so that she feels more able to achieve it. It is important to note that the ultimate goal doesn't shrink, it is your thinking about it that matters. There are somethings you can do. First, limit the initial investment in time. In our cleaning the house example, spend 30 minutes cleaning rather than five hours. The second thing is, divide the goal into smaller, manageable, bite size tasks and set progress milestones that are quickly within reach. For example, clean the small bathroom first. By doing this, your thinking about the magnitude of your challenge shifts, and you can get unstuck, stop procrastinating and begin to act. One. Step. At. A. Time.

**A deadline creates Urgency.**
One benefit of a quarterly plan is that for 12 weeks you can fiercely focus on a few vital actions that drive your results. You can't effectively pursue a large number of different things in a 12 week plan. In 12 weeks we're going to focus on the Winning Action Commitments that are most important to help you hit your goals. If planning didn't help you to achieve better, there would be no reason to plan. The whole point of planning should be to help you identify and implement the few Winning Action Commitments that you need to take to reach your chosen, current goals.
Your plan should start by identifying your 12 week goals and these must tie into your overall Vision from Chapter two. How will achieving these goals bring you closer to that vision you have for your life and work?

Once you have established your 12 week goals, we will then look at your Winning Action Commitments. The easiest way to do this is to breakdown your 12 week goal into its individual parts. Let's take some of Melissa's goals as our examples. Melissa wants to lose 20 lbs and increase her business turnover by 25%. She needs to write down her Winning Action Commitments for her income goal and for her weight loss goal separately. Her Winning Action Commitments are going to be her daily or weekly actions that have the highest impact in driving progress towards meeting these 12 week goals. 12 weeks is long enough to get things done, yet short enough to create and maintain a sense of urgency. Having focussed 12 week goals and Winning Action Commitments eliminates diffusion and procrastination and demands immediate action. It's not enough to have the intention of changing. You have to act on that intention for things to get better. Not just once, but consistently. As Bob Goff wrote in his book Becoming Love in a World full of Setbacks and Difficult People, "No one is remembered for what they only planned to do".

I want you to decide on two or maximum three goals that you are going to work on in this coming 12 weeks. Think about the categories from your wheel of life. Remember in Chapter three, we thought about how abstract goals can lead to procrastination? We're going to ensure that we write these goals in a SMART way.

Your goal needs to be
S pecific
M easurable
A stretch, yet
R ealistic and
T imebound.

Let's take Melissa's example; are her goals specific? Yes, she wants to lose 20lbs and she wants to increase her business turnover by 25% before April. Is it measurable? Yes, she can measure her weight loss in lbs lost and she can measure her business turnover in £s gained. Are they a stretch yet realistic? Well, as far as we know, Melissa is an otherwise healthy and well person, so there is no reason we know of that she can't lose 20lbs within 12 weeks, but it's still tough and requires change and discipline, so that would seem 'A stretch yet Realistic'. She's looking to increase her business turnover by 25%, she's not looking to triple or quadruple the turnover, and she's going to put in some specific actions as to how she can achieve this 25% increase, so that would seem A stretch yet Realistic. Timebound. Well, because our plan is a 12 week plan, our goals are time bound. We want to achieve these goals, or make significant progress towards them, within the next 12 weeks.


Scheduling.
It's not enough to have a vision and a plan. New actions are almost always uncomfortable, that's one of the things that makes change so difficult. It's one thing to identify your Winning Action Commitments, it is quite another to consistently do them for 12 weeks. Your current actions are creating your current results, to create new results you will have to do things differently and do different things. One problem is that your existing environment and your old triggers encourage you to continue with your old habits. A written action plan helps to create new behaviours even in the presence of your old environmental triggers. The plan creates a new set of conscious action choices that can help you to produce new results. If you consistently apply your Winning Action Commitments for 12 weeks, your goal will likely become a reality, but without structural support, following through becomes a constant battle of will power, and, as we said before, will power has a fatigue factor. As we have all experienced, sometimes we have the will power and other times we don't. This method gives you the tools and structures that can support your will power. So, whether you've got a surplus or a lack of willpower on a particular day, stick to your planned schedule. From your overall vision and your wheel of life, you decide on which areas of your life you will make your 12 week goals in. From your 12 week goals, you decide your Winning Action Commitments for those 12 weeks, and then you structure those Winning Action Commitments into a weekly and daily schedule.

### Have a Schedule, not a to-do list
Why will this help?

An open loop is a commitment that you made to yourself or someone else, but which hasn't been fulfilled yet. It can be a task or a project you started but not yet finished. It can be something really small, anything that you know you have to do but haven't done yet.

Open loops aren't restricted to your work life, they can also stem from your personal life. Relationship situations left unresolved, someone you meant to call but haven't got around to, an awkward conversation that has to happen that you keep putting off, things you need to remember like, 'must buy milk, sign permission slip for school, return that 'phone call, make dental appointment'... the list is endless. They're commitments made to yourself or to another person that haven't yet been fulfilled. They're hanging out in limbo (your brain), and they drain your energy and steal your focus without you even realising it.

The phenomenon of the 'open loop' was first discovered by psychologist and psychiatrist, Bluma Zeigarnik. She discovered what is now known as the Zeigarnik Effect (open loop), the tendency of our brain to remember and focus on incomplete tasks more than it does on completed tasks.

The Zeigarnik effect not only hinders your mind from effective productivity by distracting you with other unresolved tasks, but it also impedes your mental rest and recovery when you're not in the office by flooding your mind with thoughts of work after hours, including at bedtime.

How many times have you laid awake at night, with thoughts of unfinished tasks going around and around in your mind? No matter how much you get done in a day, your 'magic porridge pot' of a To-Do list just keeps filling up the page the again and again.

I've written before about how visualising doing something can "trick" the brain into thinking it's actually doing it. Writing something down in your schedule, against a specific time slot you've allocated for doing that task or assignment, seems to use enough of the brain to trigger this effect. You'll feel a lot calmer and more in control of your time and tasks.

What can I do about it? Action for you.

- Get a diary or planner, whether paper or electronic, that has an **hour by hour breakdown of each day**

- To close the mental loop and go to bed with a clearer, calmer mind ready for sleep, don't have a rolling to-do list of unfinished tasks; instead, write all those tasks, jobs, errands, 'phone calls, conversations, meetings, shopping trips, permission slips, into your schedule against a **specific time slot** you've allocated for doing them!

**Managing your energy**
Scheduling Sleep

"Sleep in not an optional lifestyle luxury. Sleep is a non-negotiable biological necessity. It is your life support system" Matt Walker (PhD), Neuroscientist and sleep expert.

The quality and quantity of sleep you get has a huge effect on your health concentration, cognition and wellbeing, it effects almost every other aspect of life. Notice when you procrastinate most; does it coincide with days you're short on sleep and feeling very tired? A lack of good quality sleep can cause a lack of motivation, for sure. When you're tired, your will power is low and you long for the old, familiar habits; you've done them a thousand times, they seem easy to fall back into when you're exhausted.

Sleep is your Superpower! Yet, how many of us actually schedule our sleep?

Isn't sleep one of the first things we squeeze when we're busy and need to 'find time' to do just a little more work, just one more task? Bedtime gets later and later as we frantically work against a looming deadline. Or, we pack so much busy-ness into our day, that we feel as if the only time we have to ourself, to unwind a little or to be alone, is late at night when the rest of the world sleeps. I understand, believe me! This quote from Sara C Mednick PhD resonates deeply with me; perhaps you too?

"Maybe you like the way your brain thinks when the rest of the world has stopped making so much noise, or maybe it's the only opportunity you have to control your own time. Creative people tend to be owls. My musician poet sister, Lisa Mednick, remembers feeling a kinship with the night from early on. "As a kid I stayed up past bedtime reading by flashlight and later on listening to music. I also remember waking up before it got light out and colouring with crayons before I could see the colours. All that time I was alone and not afraid of the dark. I was too young to realise it of course but I was taking advantage of the solitude and the rare chance to control my own time. For an artist that is crucial, to be able to have control over how you spend your hours. Even at the age of 6 believe it or not I think I knew that. I'm sure that is one reason why creative people train themselves, or maybe they're wired, to be awake and alive while the world, the authorities, sleep. I mean, you can work sort of outside the radar I suppose, otherwise everyone else is directing your thoughts and activities. At least that's how it can feel if you'd rather be left alone with your dreams and actually create something worth having spent your time on".

Or perhaps for you, staying awake late into the evening isn't a preference and choice. Perhaps you have anxiety or hyper arousal that keeps you awake, mind whirring, ruminating in the darkness. Or, maybe you have no trouble falling asleep, but you wake several times in the night and find it difficult to fall back to sleep. Perhaps you don't remember having trouble sleeping at all, and yet you still wake in the morning feeling exhausted and unrefreshed by your sleep.

It's important for me to make it very clear who this advice is going to be most effective for and who it is not going to be very effective for. This section is not designed for people suffering from insomnia, it is not about recommendations that will treat or cure insomnia. This section is for people who don't have clinical insomnia but would still like to try and do all they can to fine tune and optimise their sleep. If you prioritise your sleep and keep to a sleep schedule, you'll feel calmer, more well rested and clear headed and get much more done with your time during the day.

Dim Your Lights: Try to keep away from bright lights because they can hinder the production of melatonin, a hormone that the body creates to facilitate sleep.

Why will this help me?

"The daily opening and closing of our eyes to the rhythm of the sun and moon for millions of years has reinforced a strong schedule that regulates the biological and psychological processes of all living things". Scientists refer to this daily rhythm as circadian from the Latin *circa* meaning around and *dia* meaning day. This chain of action governs the sleep / wake cycle of every human, animal and plant on the planet! Isn't that amazing?

So, how does our brain and body know when to do what?

The Sun! And the specific types of light it shines.

Light is your circadian rhythm's strongest signal. Light comes in many different colours, determined by the frequency of the light's wavelengths. Within 'visible light' we can see wavelengths between 400 and 700 nanometre; with the shorter wavelengths being cooler colours, purple and blue and the longer wavelengths appearing as warmer colours red and orange, with yellow and green in the middle.

As the sun begins to rise, the blueish light of dawn enters the retina and is detected by three different types of retinal cells. Two of these, rods and cones, are used for processing visual perceptions the third, the retinal ganglion cells, (RGCs) specifically process information for the circadian system. I just think this is amazing stuff! How well designed we are!

Whereas, rods and cones can process a broad spectrum of wavelengths, RGCs pickup only blue light as this particular wavelength is what signals the brain what time it is and when to release either melatonin (the circadian rhythms main sleepy hormone) or cortisol (your energising hormone).

The RGCs send this colour information to your brain, specifically the hypothalamus, to let it know that daytime is coming. Your superchiasmatic nucleus becomes energised triggering a series of events designed to get you going so you can kick start your day.

Amongst other things, blue light triggers:
the pineal gland to stop producing sleepy melatonin
the adrenal glands to ramp up production of energising hormones such as cortisol and epinephrine your metabolic system to start heating up your body temperature.

By contrast, as the sun sets in fiery red and orange, your eyes look into the evening sky and sense impending darkness. The absence of blue light alerts the superchiasmatic nucleus to stimulate the pineal gland to start upping melatonin production for the night sending your whole system into wind down mode.

How do I know if I'm exposing myself to blue light? Well, what do you tend to spend your evening doing?

Here are some places you will find blue light:
Mobile Phone screen
Computer / laptop / tablet screen
LED lightbulbs

What can I do about it? ACTIONS FOR YOU

1. Ensure screen-free time for at least one hour (longer if practical for you) before bedtime
2. Invest in some blue light blocker glasses
3. Turn off the bright LED lights during the evening, instead the reds and oranges of candle flames are a perfect signal to your system that sleepytime is drawing near.

Spend time in blue light within the first hour of your day.

You may think after reading that previous section that blue light is all things bad, but that's not true. It hinders melatonin production and so is not helpful to you at bedtime, when you want to be sleepy, however, in the morning, when you want to wake feeling refreshed and kick start your day, blue light is your go-to!

Remember, amongst other things, blue light triggers

- the pineal gland to stop producing sleepy melatonin
- the adrenal glands to ramp up production of energising hormones such as cortisol and epinephrine
- your metabolic system to start heating up your body temperature.

What can I do about it? Actions for you

- Within the first hour of waking up in the morning, make sure you get some blue light on your face.
- If it's a bright day, go and sit outside, turn your face to the sun and soak in those blue morning hues.
- If it's dark, cold, wet or wintry, invest in a blue light alarm clock or a light box. (can be purchased at Lumie.com or similar sites). The wake-up lights are like a personal sunrise, a gradually brightening light that gently rouses you from sleep so that you feel naturally wide awake, more energised and ready for the day ahead. Light therapy is proven to put you in a better mood, boost energy and help you to feel more alert. It can also be an effective treatment for SAD (seasonal affective disorder).

Keep your bedroom cool (18 degrees C is optimum).

Why will it help me?

Sleeping in a cooler room can improve your sleep quality. Scientists link this to the fact that our body temperature naturally drops at night, hence the metabolism rate slows down, and we spend less energy during sleep. The most pronounced drop in body temperature happens when you enter REM sleep. It's the stage of deep sleep during which you typically see dreams. Cellular repair and memory consolidation occur during REM sleep too, so it's a very important stage and sleeping at cooler temperatures may promote the transition to it. A decrease in your core temperature results in increased levels of the sleep hormone melatonin. But what's even more interesting is that melatonin itself has a hypothermic effect, meaning it can decrease your temperature. A combination of these can help you get therapeutic sleep.

What can I do about it? ACTIONS FOR YOU

Invest in a mattress topper.

A mattress topper with a cooling effect creates an additional breathable layer between you and the mattress.

Improve air circulation.

Opening windows more often for ventilation can help reduce the humidity, especially if the bedroom is next to a bathroom or kitchen.

Invest in an electric fan.

If it's hot and humid outside too or if there is some reason an open window isn't an option for you; invest in an electric fan. Coming in models free standing or wall mounted, with cooling effect or without, shop around and find the right fan your bedroom.

Choose natural materials

To boost the cooling effect, opt for breathable bedding sheets and blankets made from cotton or linen. These materials don't trap heat and can absorb the sweat without feeling wet.

## Keep Your Bedtime Routine Consistent

### Why will this help?

Humans are creatures of habit. Like any other routine, bedtime routines establish habits that help our brains recognise when it's time to sleep. By performing the same activities in the same order every night, your brain comes to see those activities as a precursor to sleep.

Bedtime routines also play an important role in reducing late-night stress and anxiety — the kind of worrisome thoughts that keep you up at night. Anxious thoughts and rumination activate your mind and sympathetic nervous system. Left unchecked, these thoughts can intensify and cause sleep problems. By following a bedtime routine, you can keep your mind focused on other tasks and encourage yourself to relax instead.

Bedtime routines helps children connect with their natural circadian rhythms, learn how to calm themselves down, and practice healthy habits that promote good sleep. Bedtime routines have also been found to have profoundly positive impacts in other areas of children's lives, including better memory, mental health, and attention, and bedtime routines for adults are just as important. Bedtime routines help your brain separate the day from the night, clear your mind and body of the day's stresses, and relax into sleep.

What can I do about it?

- Your bedtime routine is a set of activities you perform in the same order, every night, in the 30 to 60 minutes before you go to bed. Bedtime routines can vary, but often include calming activities like taking a warm bath, reading, journaling, or meditation.

- Decide on a Set Bedtime and write it into your schedule. As part of your natural sleep-wake cycle, your brain starts winding down for sleep a few hours before bedtime. You can use your bedtime routine to make that process more effective. First, decide on your bed- and wake-up times, and stick to them every day. Following a consistent sleep routine helps train your brain to naturally feel tired when it's bedtime. Next, schedule a time to begin your bedtime routine every night, anywhere between 30 minutes to 2 hours before bed. Set an alarm if you need to. Write it into your schedule.

- Take a soothing soak. As part of your sleep-wake cycle, your body experiences various hormonal changes throughout the day. One of these is melatonin production, which begins in the evening to prepare you for sleep, and at the same time, your core body temperature drops.
  Scientists have found that mimicking that night time drop in body temperature via a warm bath can trigger a similarly sleepy reaction. Consider taking a warm bath about an hour before you go to sleep.
  "There's actually good science behind this," says Matthew Walker, a neuroscientist and sleep specialist at the University of California, Berkeley. "We know that your core body temperature needs to drop by about 2 to 3 degrees Fahrenheit to initiate good sleep and then maintain deep sleep. The way it works is this: For you to get your heat out of the core of your body, you actually need to release that core heat through the outer perimeter surfaces of your body, namely your hands and your feet. And this is why hot baths actually work ... for the opposite reason most people

think," Walker adds. "You get into a hot bath, you get out, you think I'm nice and toasty, I get into bed and I fall asleep better because I'm warm. The opposite is true. What happens with a bath ... is you actually bring all of the blood to the surface. And your hands and your feet are wonderful radiators of that heat. So you are essentially like a snake charmer — you are charming the heat out of the core of your body to the surface of your body."

- Stretch, Breathe, and Relax.
  Relaxation techniques like deep breathing exercises or progressive muscle relaxation (PMR) can allow you to let go of physical and mental tension, by instead focusing on your body and mindfully relaxing. Remember way back in chapter one, we discovered that long, slow, deep breathing communicates to the body you are very safe and this allows the Parasympathetic Nervous System to help you into rest and digest (or rest and repair) mode.  In case you missed it, and because it's worth repeating, here is that breathing exercise again, from chapter one.

  One simple thing you can do, anytime, anywhere to help activate your Parasympathetic Nervous System and calm your body is to *Take some slow breaths*. Try what I call 'Box and Belly Breathing'. Using your finger in the air in front of you, trace the four sides of a 'box' or square as you breathe in for 4, hold for 4, out for 4, hold for 4. If you feel you'd like to deepen further you can try in for 6, hold for 6, out for 6, hold for 6. As you do this, have your other hand placed lightly on your belly and feel your belly rise with your in-breath and fall with your out-breath.

  A daily yoga routine has been shown to improve sleep quality, and a few simple stretches or massage before bed can prevent cramping. Some light yoga, stretching, and breathing exercises can go a long way toward relaxing you into sleep. See what works for you and add it to your bedtime routine.

- Get lost in a good book (Paper book, not an e-reader)
  There's an age-old reason why reading a book in bed is part of so many children's night time routines: reading puts us in the right headspace for a good night's sleep.
  Similarly to how physical exercise strengthens the body, cognitive exercises — like reading — are important to strengthen the mind. Strong cognitive function can help reduce mental chatter, which in turn, helps us drop into a quiet state of relaxation.

Reading a book or actively listening to a story are two ways to keep the mind engaged.

The act of engaging our imaginations with a paperback allows us to enter an altered state of consciousness. While our mind is quite literally lost in the words, our body gets the chance to rest and relax. And when the body is more relaxed, it becomes easier for us to wind down and drift off.

Eat more foods rich in Magnesium.

Why will this help me?

In order to fall asleep and stay asleep, your body and brain need to relax. On a chemical level, magnesium aids this process by activating the parasympathetic nervous system. First, magnesium regulates neurotransmitters, which send signals throughout the nervous system and brain. It also regulates the hormone melatonin, which guides sleep-wake cycles in your body. Second, this mineral binds to gamma-aminobutyric acid (GABA) receptors. GABA is the neurotransmitter responsible for quieting down nerve activity. By helping to quiet the nervous system, magnesium may help prepare your body and mind for sleep.

If you're not getting enough magnesium, then you may experience sleep problems.

What can I do about it? ACTIONS FOR YOU

Include more of these magnesium rich foods in your daily diet for better quantity and quality of sleep:

Dark chocolate
Avocados
Nuts
Legumes
Tofu
Seeds
Whole grains
Fatty fish
Bananas
Leafy greens

Get to the shops and stock up today to start seeing improvements sooner!

If you have had a poor or interrupted night's sleep and are finding it difficult to feel calm and productive and stay on schedule the following day, try the following to help you get through the day until bedtime.

- Hydrate, hydrate, hydrate. Your brain and nervous system send out electrical signals to function properly. Having a regular supply of water will help to increase electrical functioning in your brain for clearer thinking, so you will feel more efficient and productive.
- Take regular movement breaks. Taking scheduled breaks is important whenever you're working, but it's essential to make most of your limited energy when tired. I know it sounds a little counterproductive — why should you expend precious energy on exercise when work needs to get done? While you're definitely spending some energy on moving, it also has an invigorating effect. If you're somewhere you can put on your favourite song and dance around, do it! Get the benefit of movement and the feel good factor of your favourite tune. If you can't do that, the main thing is to stand up and move a little bit.
- Don't give in to the sugar cravings. We crave carb and sugar laden snacks when we haven't slept long or well enough is because our body is searching for quick and easy energy to help us feel like we have more energy, but you'll feel better if you don't give in! When you eat any form of sugar or simple carbohydrate, especially if not accompanied by protein, fat or fibre, it is digested and absorbed very fast, causing your blood sugar to spike. The body then releases insulin to process the blood sugar, but often it will drive the blood sugar level down too far. Then you produce cortisol, the stress hormone, to drive your blood sugar back up, and you also crave sugar and carbs, starting the cycle all over again. This is the blood-sugar roller-coaster.

The occasional poor night of sleep happens to us all, but wherever possible, take the steps to schedule your sleep routine and treat sleep like the superpower it is! If you're serious about taking back control of your time, getting more done in less time and being present to enjoy each moment, you're going to need to manage your energy and get good sleep!

**Managing your energy**
Scheduling Meals

"I need to eat healthily. I know what I need to do to eat healthily. So why do I keep not doing it?"

The knowledge to performance gap is what psychologists call it. You need to make it easier to do your intended action, than not to do it.

If you've planned to eat a protein packed homemade egg salad for lunch but you haven't prepped it at all, or allowed yourself time to prep it, but you have however got a kitchen cupboard full of your favourite instant, processed, pre-packaged lunchtime snacks, guess what you're more likely to eat for lunch?

Write meal times and meal preparation time into your daily planner! If you write it down and schedule time in for it, you are far more likely to do it than if you don't write it into your daily plan. You might think egg salad is super quick to make, but it still takes some time. How long? 10 minutes? 15? Time yourself and get accurate about how much meal prep time to schedule into your daily plan. It's no good being in a client call until 12.30pm and then scheduling only time to eat lunch, not make it, before your next appointment. You'll end up in that pre-packaged processed instant snack cupboard and back at your desk before you know what's happened, or you'll end up skipping lunch altogether. Do you do that sometimes? You've got an uber busy day, back to back with tasks and meetings that all seem to overrun. You just haven't had time for lunch. So, how's your energy by mid-afternoon? I'd wager it's flagging! It's such a common mistake that busy women repeat time and again, but it won't help you get more done in the long run. That 30 minutes you 'saved' by not stopping for lunch, you'll need to take back double later on. This might be in the form of being so hungry by 4pm you can't put it off any longer and stop to eat anyway. It might be that, (like I did for years) you suffer headaches and if you skip lunch, then by 4pm you can no longer sit in front of a screen or hold a coherent conversation but have to go and lie down in a dark room. It might be that, determined to get through your 'magic porridge pot' of a To-Do list today, you do push on through hunger, thirst and general low energy malaise only to find at a later date the 'work' you completed was riddled with errors, typos and mistakes you hadn't noticed at the time, and you have to spend time amending it. Honestly, that 30 minutes you think you save by skipping lunch, will always demand repayment with interest so you may as well schedule in lunch on your terms, make time to eat well and enjoy it and have better energy and alertness to carry you through the afternoon.

The same goes for all your meals; you want to eat well, schedule in time to prepare your healthy breakfast. Don't have time in the mornings? Can you schedule time to prep it the night before? Remember, the idea is to make it as easy as possible for you to do your planned action, in this case to eat a healthy meal, and that begins at the point of shopping. Fill your fridge and cupboards with the type of foods you plan to eat, have them readily available, easily to hand.

**Managing your energy**
Water Intake

This is another area where busy find it difficult to consistently achieve what they plan to do. However much water you personally strive to drink per day, I know very few busy women who make their total daily! Finding it hard to concentrate? Do you have brain-fog? Afternoon fatigue? It could well be that you're not drinking enough water. Water is essential for life, it's essential to maintain the structure of our cells, aid regulation of our body temperature, maintain our blood volume, aid metabolism, assist in all digestion and absorption functions. Without water, we do not survive.

Aim to drink two litres of water a day. You may drink more on a day big on exercise and less on a particularly sedentary day. More on a hot day, less on a cool day. For me personally, I know that if I want to make my two litres for the day, I need to have drunk half a litre by 9.30am and be at one and a half litres by 1.30pm. Then the rest just seems to follow naturally by 6pm. However, if I miss those water milestones early in the day, I don't tend to catch up and the day goes awry, often ending with me feeling below par and low on energy.

Get yourself a bottle that suits you and take it everywhere! I mean everywhere. Mine is 500ml, so I know once I've had four of them, I've done it. You can get many different types that mark off your water milestones on the bottle, either in millilitres or in times of day. Find what suits you, write your water milestones into your daily planner and aim for them.

**Scheduling Exercise**

Remember, we want to make it as easy as possible for you to do your planned actions. Let's talk about exercise. Regular exercise is another area of life that seems to often get dropped when life feels too hectic. Many women I work with enjoy exercising and tell me they always feel better for it afterwards, and yet, it's often something that they plan to do, but end up not doing because they 'didn't have time'.

When's a good time of day for you to work out?

A good time of day for you to work out is when you know you're most likely to pay the cost and stick to it! If you know you're more likely to pay the cost of losing an extra hour in bed in the morning in order to get up and work out; that's the best time for you! If you know you're more likely to pay the cost of missing your favourite TV programme in the evening to work out, and likely to hit snooze and not get up early to work out, then, for you, an evening workout wins out because you're more likely to actually do it. There are no results or health benefits to scheduling a workout regularly, only to actually *doing* one regularly!

That said, if high intensity exercise is your thing, (think HIIT, spin, step aerobics), evening is not necessarily the best time for this.

Evening is a good time for low intensity exercise such as yoga, Pilates, Chi Gong, or Tai Chi. Low intensity exercise involving breathwork and gentle stretching activate the parasympathetic nervous system and can aid relaxation and sleep.
For your high intensity exercise and cardio, earlier in your day is better than when you're winding down for bed.

Dress for the job you want.
If you've scheduled your work out for the morning, why would you not get up and dress in your work out clothes? I often speak with mums who get up and dressed for the school run and then when they get home again, intending to work out, they don't feel like it. A cup of coffee is calling. They don't want to get changed and go out for a run now. Well, dress for the job you want! Get up, dress straight away in your work out gear, do the school run that way, (nobody is going to mind believe me, if anything they'll just be jealous you're off to work out when they 'can't' fit it in to their day). That way, as soon as the school run is over, pass go and go directly to the gym / for your run. You don't even have to go back into the house, no getting changed, no call of the coffee and sofa. Get up, get dressed, work out. Then you can shower, change and *treat* yourself to that post-workout coffee if you still fancy it.

Get a work out buddy.
If you can buddy up with a friend and work out together, fabulous! There's nothing to keep us as accountable as one another! You're a lot less likely, (7 times less likely actually), to cancel on a friend than to cancel on yourself! If you still feel you both need even more incentive to keep that exercise commitment, then swap gym clothes with each other the night before. This way, if you cancel, your buddy can't exercise because you have her gear and vice-versa!
Remember: Make it easier to stick to the action you've committed to, than not to.

**Inconsistency and the intention iceberg**

Do you remember when we talked about Covey's Quadrant? We looked at focused time and reactive time, and we looked at time blocking into our daily schedule. Putting in those reactive times and those blocks of focused time, as well as the other daily necessities such as sleep time, personal care time, commuting or travelling time, client appointments, networking meetings, the school runs, meal times and the other things you need to fit into your days. We said then that those blocks of focused times would be filled up with your Winning Action Commitments.

There are other reasons we appear to be procrastinating, or be inconsistent with completing our planned Winning Action Commitments. Let's look at Conscious and Unconscious Intentions. If you think of your intentions as an iceberg, part of the iceberg is visible above sea level, but there is another part of it that you can't see from the surface, hidden below the waterline.

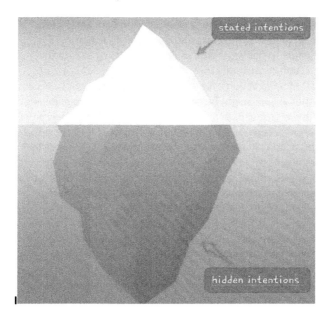

It's the same with your conscious and unconscious intentions. We all have conscious stated intentions, so going back to one of Melissa's examples, she has stated her intention to lose 20lbs. This is her conscious intention; the part of her intention that she is aware of. But often we have unconscious intentions too and sometimes these are in conflict with our conscious stated intentions. This can be one of the things that holds us back from achieving our goals. Here is some of the unconscious intentions that might affect Melissa's ability to carry through her plan to lose 20lbs.

- I don't want to give up the enjoyment of some of my favourite foods.
- I don't want to get out of my warm bed to go running in cold weather.
- I don't want to expend the effort.
- Maybe this is just the weight I'm meant to be now I'm this age.
- I don't have enough time.

Being aware of and exploring our unconscious intentions can help us acknowledge them and not give in to them.

Every winning action commitment you decide to commit to will come at a cost. So, before I ask you to choose your Winning Action Commitments, we're going to count the cost. I want you to think about all the actions that can have a big impact on helping you reach your goals. Remember, we are not going to do all of these actions.

We're just going to think about all the actions you could take to achieve these goals and which are the ones that you think will have the biggest impact and move you furthest towards attaining your goals. Write them down. Get them down on paper; a plan on paper is so much more effective than a plan between your ears! Next, we're going to look at the costs of these Winning Action Commitments. What will it cost you if you are going to take this winning action consistently for the next 12 weeks? Some actions might be repeated actions, for example, working out four times a week. Other actions might be one off actions, for example, joining a gym or fitness group. But whether you're taking this action as a one off or daily or weekly or several times a week, what is the cost to you of this action? Remember our intention iceberg? The cost to you is not just a cost in money, will it cost you getting up earlier out of bed in the morning? Will it cost you your comfort? Will it cost you some time that you would usually spend watching TV to go and exercise instead? What will you have to say no to in order to continue to say yes to this winning action over the next 12 weeks? Think about all the costs you might have to pay if you're seriously going to commit to doing this one winning action consistently for 12 weeks. Write these down too.

Those high impact Winning Action Commitments that you've decided you're willing to pay the cost for are going to be your Winning Action Commitments for the next 12 weeks.

If you successfully complete those Winning Action Commitments consistently for 12 weeks, it is very likely that you will achieve your goals.

Something else to be aware of when you make any big change in your life is the Emotional Cycle of Change . It's helpful to understand the process we humans go through emotionally when we try to implement any big change in our life. If we understand it, we are less likely to allow it to derail us. Psychologists Don Kelly and Daryl Connor described this in a paper called the Emotional Cycle of Change . Kelly and Connor's ECOC includes five stages of emotional experience. This is the process that all people go through whenever they try to make big changes in their lives. This can be a new relationship, a new job, a move to a new town or implementing a new relationship with your time. The emotional cycle of change is always the same. Sometimes it takes longer, sometimes it's shorter, but we each go through this emotional experience when we try to make a big change in our life.

# The Emotional Cycle of Change

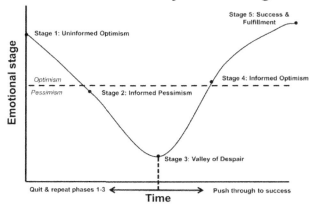

9

Stage one is uninformed optimism. You're just starting out, enthused and raring to go! This is often the most exciting stage as you're imagining all the benefits of this change you're about to make, but you have not yet had to experience any of the costs.

As you start to implement the change you move into stage two, informed pessimism. The benefits of the change don't seem as real or immediate, and the costs of the change are beginning to become apparent as you try to implement unfamiliar ways of doing things and new habits. You start to question if this change is really worth the effort.

The third stage is the valley of despair. This is when most people give up. You're feeling all the pain of change and the benefits seem far away and less important to you. Temptingly, there is a fast, easy way to end your discomfort; going back to the way you used to do things! If you throw in the towel when you're in the valley of despair, you go back to the first stage, uninformed optimism, which certainly feels better to you in the short term, (remember that short-term mood repair?) But it is precisely at this stage, the valley of despair, when holding fast to your compelling vision and big why is essential. Nearly all of us have had times in our lives when we wanted something so badly we were willing to do almost anything and overcome any hurdle to get it. This is why it's so important to keep connecting to your vision and big why. (Did you notice in Melissa's letter, she doesn't refer at all to her vision or big why. Maybe she skipped over that exercise? She's going to need to go back and complete it if she wants to achieve her goals).

The fourth stage is informed optimism. You're creeping back into the positive emotional area of the cycle. The benefits of your actions

---

9 Credit: Don Kelly and Daryl Connor

are starting to pay off and the costs of change are lessened because now your new actions are becoming more familiar and routine.

The final stage is success and fulfilment. At this stage, the benefits of your new actions are fully experienced, and the costs of the change have virtually gone because your new actions have become routine, familiar actions to you now. At the beginning they were difficult and uncomfortable, but now you can complete them with ease. They have become automatic.

Being aware of and acknowledging this cycle can help us be compassionate and understanding towards ourselves and others who are finding change tough, it can help us encourage and support one another and speak to ourself with kindness and understanding.

I've certainly ridden this roller-coaster myself over the past three years; my son starting his new school, selling my home and achieving my vision of moving to live by the sea. Please don't think I'm doing this alone, I couldn't do this without the encouragement, support and practical help I'm receiving from family and friends. Even so, there are certainly days I've been in that valley and I'm sure they'll be more of those over the coming years. Regularly connecting with my vision and big why is so important to keep me going. If you don't get into the habit of regularly and routinely connecting to your vision and big why, you won't think to reach for it when you need it, when times are tough. You can't use it only in emergencies; you need to 'train for the trial you're not yet in'; build the habit of making time to connect with it routinely and then, when you're in that valley, it will come to you, it will spring to your mind and sustain you. Honestly, the number of times I have been in that valley, exhausted, depleted, wondering if this is really all worth it or whether I could just go back to a saner school run closer to home, and then something has happened or been said or done to bring that vision sharply into focus again, to make it abundantly clear that the benefits my son is experiencing far outweigh this cost I'm feeling at present, is magical! Hold your vision close and connect regularly.

Booby traps to avoid:

- Your twelve week goals and actions do not align with your long term vision. It's important that your 12 week goals and plan are aligned with your longer term vision. When you set your goals, be certain they are connected to your vision.
- You aren't staying focused. Focus is critical. If you establish too many goals, you end up with too many priorities and too many Winning Action Commitments to effectively complete. Everything cannot be a priority. You will need to say no to some things in order to achieve progress at the things that matter most at this time. It takes courage to fiercely focus on a few key areas.

Keys to success:

- Keep it simple. The task of planning can run away with you if you're not careful. Don't overcomplicate it. Focus on your few key priorities for the next 12 weeks and the Winning Action Commitments that will move you towards those goals.
- Make it meaningful. Your plan should be a bit of a stretch for you. If you can do it with ease with your current actions, you're not going to make the progress you want to. You must build your plan around the things that are most important to you or there won't be the emotional resilience to keep you going when times get tough. If your plan isn't meaningful to you, you will struggle to carry it through.

**Chapter Five.**

**Neutral measuring, Imposter Syndrome and Self-Compassion, lead and lag indicators**

In this chapter we're going to explore measuring and how we measure whether we're doing what we say we are going to do or not. Measuring is something that many of us shy away from; it can be uncomfortable to be accountable. If we find that's the case, perhaps we have misunderstood the concept of accountability.

The idea of measuring your actions, your achievements or outcomes, or pinning down and scrutinizing whether you've kept to your commitments can be very emotive for a lot of people. Sometimes these things have negative connotations from school or from parents; you think you won't measure up, you're not good enough, you're going to get told off, you haven't done as you intended, or you should feel ashamed.

Despite external evidence of their abilities those experiencing 'impostor syndrome' remain convinced that they are frauds and do not deserve all they have achieved. They find it hard to believe their ability has played a role in their success and attribute any success instead to luck. To counter these feelings you might end up working harder and holding yourself to ever higher standards or avoid measuring your performance altogether.

Here are two women who identify as suffering with Imposter Syndrome.

Meryl Streep "You think, "Why would anyone want to see me again in a movie? And I don't know how to act anyway, so why am I doing this?""

Maya Angelo "I have written eleven books but each time I think 'Uh-oh they're going to find out now. I've run a game on everybody and they're going to find me out'".

Leading impostor syndrome researcher Dr Valerie young describes five main types of impostors in her 2011 book "The secret thoughts of successful women; Why capable people suffer from imposter syndrome and how to thrive in spite of it".

These 'competence types' as she calls them reflect your internal beliefs around what competency means to you.

The perfectionist.
You focus primarily on how you do things, often to the point where you demand perfection of yourself in every aspect of life. Perfection isn't a realistic goal, you can't meet these high standards. Instead of acknowledging the hard work you've put in you might criticise yourself for small mistakes and feel ashamed of what you perceive as failure. You may avoid trying new things if you believe you can't do them perfectly.

The natural genius.
You pick up new skills with very little effort and believe you should understand things and processes straight away. Your belief that competent people can handle anything with little difficulty leads you to feel like a fraud when you have a hard time. If something doesn't come easily to you, you might feel ashamed or embarrassed.

The rugged individualist or soloist.
You believe you should be able to handle everything solo. If you can't achieve success independently you consider yourself unworthy. Asking someone for help or accepting support when it's offered doesn't just mean failing your own high standards it also means admitting your inadequacies and showing yourself as a failure.

The expert.
Before you can consider your work a success you want to learn everything there is to know on the topic. You might spend so much

time pursuing your quest for more information that you end up having to devote more time to your main task

The superhero.
You link competence to your ability to succeed in every role you hold, whether student, friend, employee, parent or spouse failing to successfully navigate the demands of these roles simply proves, in your opinion, your inadequacy. Then you push yourself to the limit, expending as much energy as possible in every role. Even this maximum effort may not resolve your impostor feelings, you might think you should be able to do more or that it should feel easier.

True impostor feelings involve self-doubt, uncertainty about your talents and abilities and a sense of unworthiness that doesn't align with what others think about you.

Do you find yourself thinking "I wish I could have her confidence, look at her she's got it all together she's got it really sorted, I wish I could be like that." Then maybe you overhear that same person in conversation saying "Gosh, I was so nervous, I felt so unsure about that, I'm really glad you liked it because I was so worried about it". Have you had that moment of realising "Wow even her? Even that woman who I thought really had it all together and had it sorted, is carrying around those worries and insecurities as well!" We just don't know everyone's story, and so many people carry these around.

Something else common is that feeling of "I know this so surely everyone else must already know it too. What have I got to say that they don't already know?" When you know your subject really well it can seem so simple and straight forward to you because you're so familiar with it you assume other people must know it too. A big part of what you can do is to remember that you bring value, you really do bring value. Everybody doesn't know, what you know about your particular field of expertise and there are some great things you can do to remind yourself of the value that you truly bring.

When do you feel these sort of this impostor feelings? Is it when you're doing what you love?
When you're in your zone of genius? I'd lay money that it isn't!
Does it tend to happen when you're working on your business rather than in your business? When you're planning to do something new or different? Branching out? Putting yourself out there?
You start looking at some of your competitors, researching, and their websites and their social media and suddenly you start getting that tightening in your tummy and that sinking feeling, telling yourself "they're doing that and they're doing that and why aren't I doing it like that? Mine doesn't look like that!"

### Comparison is the thief of joy

**"A flower does not think of competing with the flower next to it, it just blooms".**

### What can I do about it?

Read your testimonials. I know how easy it is when you do start going down that rabbit hole of looking at everybody else's fabulous website and social media posts and blogs and starting to feel really inadequate but comparison truly does steal your joy. Don't compare. Remember the value you bring to your clients. There's a really good way to do this, go read your testimonials! Go and read what your clients have said about you and the value that you've brought to them and the difference that you've made to them! Remind yourself of that value that you're bringing.

One way that I really like to think about it is this; Jeans.

When we find a really good pair of jeans that fit us really well, the right pair that hug in all the right places and feel just great and make you feel amazing, that's your pair of jeans! Your favourite pair of jeans, you love them. I don't think any of us women would ever say to somebody "I need a new pair of jeans, next time you go to the supermarket can you just take some cash buy me a pair of jeans, any pair, about size 10 to 12, just get me a pair of blue jeans". None of us would do that, because we don't just want a pair of jeans it has to be the right fit for us, it has to be exactly what we need to make us feel good! It's the same with you, whatever industry you are in, whatever offer or product or service you are giving and providing. People want to connect with the right person for them, someone who's going to talk their language and work with them in the way that they want to work and gel. So in the way you bring your offer you've got your uniqueness. You've got the things that make you deliver your offer in a way that nobody else can!

Accept that you have some role in your success! Look at where you are now, you have something to do with how you got there! It didn't just happen to you, it's happened because of you. You've put in that work, that effort, you've gained that knowledge, you've brought that value to others. Accept that you play a role in your success and give yourself some gratitude for that. Just like you would be thankful to somebody else and you would give them gratitude, give yourself some acknowledgement that you play a role in your success and getting you to where you are now.

Remember that being wrong doesn't make you a fake. This will happen sometimes. There will be times where something will go wrong or you'll have a set back and if you're already feeling that kind of impostor syndrome and that lack of confidence in yourself, that can sometimes be enough to make you say to yourself, "See I was right, I shouldn't be doing this. I got that wrong didn't I". Just because you get something wrong or make a mistake or something doesn't go as you planned, don't let that tell you that therefore you don't own your place here in your field of expertise. We can do this with a lot of things in our life and this is emotional reasoning. One common example of emotional reasoning is when we're working very hard and we start to actually tell ourselves that we want to pace ourselves now, to take some breaks, to do some self-care. We start feeling guilty for slowing down, guilty for taking that break, and emotional reasoning then lies to us "if you feel guilty for taking a rest then it must be bad, it must be bad to rest" or even worse, "if you feel guilty for taking that rest then you must be lazy, you're not being productive enough". That isn't true, that is our emotion trying to put something on to us which isn't true and the same can happen when you get something wrong. You make one mistake, you have one failure or one set back an emotional reasoning lies to you "there you go you see, you weren't good enough, told you so". Don't let that emotional reasoning win because that isn't a fact. That isn't the truth. That is something that your emotions are playing on in your mind. Remind yourself that you do know what you're talking about and none of us have built our businesses and other things in our lives without some setbacks along the way. Nobody has a straight path, we all have meanders in our river as we go.

**The importance of Self Compassion**

Busting a Myth

I was surprised to discover in some spheres, the concept of self-care and self-compassion has been badly misunderstood and misinterpreted and I thought, maybe others are labouring under this same misapprehension, so I think it's worth addressing here.

I was shocked to read one author write "it demands we worship the god-of-self; a merciless ruler that will stop at nothing to get the service it craves." "It encourages people to do what feels good, and removes restrictions and responsibility to others. It values self-love over sacrifice, self-care over service and self-interest over selflessness".

This could not be more wrong.

Self-love is not about doing whatever you want and whatever feels good in the moment, that way lies procrastination, weight gain, instant gratification, debt, the list goes on.

It's compassion, for others *and* for self. Valuing others as you value yourself. Loving your neighbour as you love yourself. Recognising, the beauty you see in others is in you too! The divine in me, honours the divine in you. It's my view that there really isn't a difference between compassion for self and compassion for others, it's just that we usually exclude ourselves from the circle of compassion. And, if we're trying to help another while standing outside that circle of compassion ourselves, it can actually come off as pretty condescending. Are we thinking well of ourselves because we're being so generous and giving while thinking nothing of our own needs? Are we denying we have the same needs as others? Setting ourselves up as some sort of super-human? That certainly doesn't give the other person an opportunity to reciprocate and may feel to them like receiving charity from you, rather than connectedness, friendship and kindness. When we include ourself in that circle of compassion, when we recognise we need to nurture ourself as well as others and fill our cup too, so we have something to pour out for others. We can be of service from a place of connection with others, of recognising we're all human, all struggling together, I have something of value to offer you and you have something of value to offer me. It makes it easier to receive compassion, help and support from others as well as to give it, when you recognise we're all in that circle together, you're not standing apart, somewhere higher, looking down at others from outside.

### The importance of Self Compassion

When you have an experience of compassion for another person what goes on? What are the elements that comprise this compassionate experience? Well, the first is actually that you have to notice that suffering is occurring.

Let's say you are walking to work down the street and there is a homeless person sitting on the street corner who obviously looks like they're having a tough time. Some days you might just walk past or not even notice them on your way to work because you're in a rush, but one day for whatever reason you do notice and you notice that tis person is really struggling and then the next response, if it's a compassionate one, is it your heart goes out to them. You have some emotional response to their pain. Importantly, there's another element to compassion that shouldn't be overlooked and that is recognition of their humanity and your humanity and that we are all vulnerable. Not pitying them, not looking down on them, but remembering, there but for the grace of God go I. We are all potentially capable of finding ourselves in a situation like that.

Self-compassion has those same three elements;

Notice suffering is occurring,
A compassionate emotional response,
Recognition of shared humanity.

The idea is of being kind and emotionally responsive to your own suffering. Sadly most of us are not kind to ourselves, most of us are very judgmental and critical of ourselves, very hard on ourselves. Stop and check in with yourself and think about what you just said to yourself last time you made a mistake or felt you failed in some way. Then consider would you say that to someone you cared about? To a friend? More often than not the answer is no. We tend to speak more harshly and even cruelly to ourselves than to anyone else in our lives. Not only does that cause a lot of pain it also takes away this great coping mechanism we have, which is our ability to soothe and comfort ourselves.

In self kindness we actively treat ourselves with care and understanding rather than harsh judgement. We treat ourselves like we would a good friend, we're there for ourselves when needed.

Recognising that our imperfection, the fact that we fail and make mistakes, the fact that we suffer in life, is part of the shared human experience, it's something that we all go through. This is important, because often what happens when we notice something about ourself we don't like or something difficult happens in our life, we feel like something has gone wrong, this is abnormal in some way but actually, it's normal to be imperfect, it's normal for your life to be imperfect and when you can remember that you can actually feel more connected to your fellow humans when things go wrong as opposed to feeling isolated, and isolation is the more common experience when we feel inadequate in some way.

Firstly though, we need mindfulness. Mindfulness entails turning toward painful emotions and being willing to sit with them. To be with them without immediately trying to change them and chase them away. We need mindfulness to be able to notice when we're suffering. If you're trying to avoid suffering or fight against it and resist it, we can't open to it, just like that homeless woman on the side of the street we have to be willing to look at her and acknowledge she's really hurting. We have to be able to do that for ourselves as well. On the other hand we don't want to exaggerate the pain either, we don't want to run away with a dramatic storyline of how bad things are. Mindfulness sees our situation just as it is, no more and no less.

When we're in the role of self-critic, we're often completely consumed by that role, we don't even stop to realise the incredible pain we're causing ourselves. Perhaps the reason for our pain isn't coming from our self-criticism but is instead due to some very difficult situation. Maybe you've had a car accident for instance; we typically go straight into problem solving mode in those situations, making phone calls, who do I have to call, how do I fix this, without first stopping, and pausing to say "that was really difficult, I'm struggling with this emotionally".

Can you imagine if you had a friend who came to you and said she'd just totalled her car, what is the first thing you would do? Maybe give her comfort, show her you care, reassure her, check how she's feeling, is she hurt? That's usually our natural response to other people, to comfort them when they're hurting, but it's not the case with ourself, often that's because we aren't even tuned into our own suffering.

I'd like to lead you through a little exercise to get a sense of what self-compassion feels like and also what the lack of self-compassion feels like.

Take a couple of slow, deep breaths to start, just settle into your body and close your eyes.

I'd like you to put your hands in front of you and clench your fists really hard. Really tight. Just hold that there for a few seconds. While your fists are clenched, what do you feel? Are any emotions coming up for you?

Release your fists now and gently move your hands so your palms open and are facing upward. Do you feel a shift? What's coming up for you now?

Then place one hand on top of the other bring them firmly and yet gently over the centre of your chest, your heart space. Feel the warmth of your hands, your chest rising and falling beneath them. Just feel it. What is that feeling like for you now?

The first posture when we clenched our fists was a good metaphor for what self-criticism feels like. It feels stressful, feels painful, it feels uncomfortable, tight and rigid and that's our attitude toward ourselves when we criticise ourselves especially harshly.

Then when we open our hands most people feel a great sense of relief, a freedom, a feeling of spaciousness and that's a very good metaphor for mindfulness or just allowing things to be as they are.

Then when we put both hands over our heart, this usually feels pretty good, feels comforting, it feels warm, caring, tender and that's what self-kindness feels like. We're giving ourselves what we really want, really need.

These two different ways of relating to ourselves either with harsh self-criticism or with compassion, actually have different physiological underpinnings. All self-criticism does is it taps into our threat defence system, our fight, flight or freeze response, the amygdala the oldest part of our brain that tells us if there's a danger. Remember, we talked about this back in chapter one. This system says be prepared to fight or be prepared to run. When triggered that releases cortisol and adrenaline and it activates the sympathetic nervous system and it says 'get ready there's danger'. This system was very helpful to us evolutionarily because if a lion's chasing you, you better be prepared to do something about it if you want to survive. These days most of the time we aren't physically threatened but our self-concept is threatened. Whenever we perceive we fail or we see something about ourselves we don't like it's almost as if our self-concept is under siege, we react as if our very self was under siege and that's partly why we can be so hard on ourselves because we're trying to get rid of the threat and in a way we see the threat as our imperfect self. So, although self-criticism is painful and can cause us to be stressed and unhappy, we also don't want to be hard on ourselves for being self-critical because what the threat defence system is doing is actually trying to keep us safe. When we do notice some shortcoming we have, the reason our threat defence system is activated sometimes, not always but sometimes, there really is a problem that needs to be addressed, some way in which we aren't being our best. So even though its techniques may be very clumsy, self-criticism is trying at its heart to keep us safe, it's just not very effective.

To balance this, we have another another evolved system designed to keep us safe and that's the mammalian caregiving system. What makes mammals different than reptiles is that mammalian young are born very immature and in order for them to become mature enough to survive on their own the parents, usually the mother, have to care for them, instinctually want to care for them, to soothe and comfort and keep them warm and conversely the infant has to be physiologically programmed to be able to be soothed comforted. Tender touch and soft vocal tones, these were all triggers that were evolved to make us feel safe and secure and when this happens we release oxytocin and other sorts of opiates, we activate the parasympathetic nervous system which is designed to calm us down and make us feel safe. So when we give ourselves compassion we're actually moving our sense of safety from the threat defence system to our own caregiving and attachment system and this is much more productive. The threat defence system and the self-criticism end up making us stressed and anxious and not in a good emotional mindset to really complete anything. When we give ourselves compassion, we feel safe, we feel emotionally balanced, we feel accepted and we feel loved and this actually puts us on the best footing to not only be happy but to reach our goals.

We tend to spend a lot of time thinking about how to relate to our weaknesses, how to 'improve' ourselves. It's hard to relate to our mistakes and failures with compassion but believe it or not sometimes I think it's even harder to relate to our strengths and successes with loving kindness.

Most of us find it's much easier to think about what's wrong with ourselves than what's right, do you agree? For example, if you get an annual review at work or some sort of evaluation what do you remember most, the words of praise or if there are any slight criticisms? In fact whenever we receive the slightest negative feedback we tend to fixate on it, but when we receive a compliment it often just bounces right off us. It's often easier focusing on our weaknesses and inadequacies, in some ways we're comfortable with them, they're familiar, and I wonder if also we're afraid of feeling arrogant. We're afraid of letting that praise, letting those feelings about the ways in which were good, our strengths, make our heads swell. So then, how do we feel good about ourselves in a way that's healthy, without falling into the trap of constantly pursuing high self-esteem? We can do this by appreciating our good qualities with loving kindness and if you think about it, too much humility is not kind. If you have a good friend would you never compliment them, would you never praise them, would you never tell them what you like about them? Of course not, that would be taking them for granted and yet don't we often take ourselves for granted?

We know the main components of self-compassion are mindfulness, common humanity and kindness and I think these can be applied to our strengths as well as our weaknesses. First we have to be mindfully aware of our strengths, we have to notice them, we can't take them for granted. In order to be kind to ourselves we have to allow ourselves to voice appreciation and gratitude for what's good about ourselves, the key is we need to do it all in the context of common humanity. It's not being arrogant it is just remembering that everybody has strengths as well as weaknesses, that's also part of the shared human condition, so when we appreciate our own beauty, we can do so not because we're better than others but because every human being has beautiful qualities too.

As Kristen Neff says "Your playing small does not serve the world, there is nothing enlightened about shrinking so that other people won't feel insecure around you. We are all meant to shine, as we let our light shine we unconsciously give other people permission to do the same".


I'd like to take you through another short exercise.

I'd like you to close your eyes and drop into your body, take two or three deep breaths, settle into your body. Take a moment to think about two or three things you really like and appreciate about yourself. No embarrassment needed. What do you like about yourself? What are your strengths? If more than two or three things come up, wonderful. What do you really, really deep down appreciate about yourself? See if you can actually savour these positive qualities, let yourself soak it in. Now I'd like you to consider are there any other people that you want to appreciate for these good qualities who helped you develop them? Maybe your parents or a teacher? Or even any experiences? They are also part of who you are, they helped shape you. Send them some gratitude and appreciation as well.

Thinking Shift

We need to address the thinking shift. I'd like you to get rid of the idea that measuring is bad or negative, because actually measuring itself is just completely neutral. It's not good or bad, it just is. Measuring is your feedback loop, it's simply telling you whether what you're currently doing is working for you or not.

How many times do we decide, for example, "I'm going to lose 10lbs". What do I need to do to lose 10lbs? I decide to do sixty minutes of cardio three times a week plus twenty minutes of weights twice a week, I decide to meal plan in advance and buy only the food that's on my chosen plan, eat a maximum of 1,500 calories a day, no snacks, and to allow extra time to prepare my healthy meals.

After a while I hop on my scales and I'm aghast. I ask myself "Why isn't it working? Why aren't I losing the weight?" I think I'm doing the things I said I was going to do.  But actually, if I'm not prepared to measure and scrutinise whether I really am sticking to what I said I was going to do, how can I be sure I am successfully carrying out those actions I've identified as Winning Actions to help me lose weight and get fitter?

 I said I was going to have maximum 1,500 calories a day. I think I'm doing that, but have I actually measured? No, I haven't measured and then it turns out I'm not sticking to that at all. I was specific about what exercise I was going to do and for how long, how many times per week. Have I actually stuck to that or not?  Often, it's not that our planned actions aren't working effectively, it's that we're not actually doing those actions we planned to do. What do we find ourselves doing next? "Well, this clearly isn't working for me, I'll change the plan". So, we start a different diet or different exercise regime. Does that sound familiar?

With neutral measuring, it's about checking in on those winning action commitments and checking to what extent you're completing them. You've gone to the effort of expending your energy, identifying things you want to commit to doing, you've checked you're willing to pay the cost, if we now leave it at that and we don't measure if we're actually doing them or not, you will probably end up wondering why you are busy, busy busy, but not getting any closer to achieving your goals.

Measurement doesn't have to be complicated, it just has to be effective. The best measurement systems include two things, lead indicators and lag indicators. Your lead indicators are about tracking your progress as you go along. Your lag indicator is something that lags behind the things that you do each week. So if we stick with the losing 10lbs example, the total weight goal of losing 10lbs would be your lag indicator because it happens at the end. That weight loss is going to lag behind the actions, but a lead indicator or lead measure will be things that you agreed to do each day or each week, so for example, the number of calories per day or the number of times you're going to workout per week, have you swum the number of lengths you said you would or run the number of miles you said you would; those are your lead indicators because you can measure them as you go along.

What we're measuring in our weekly accountability and support power up sessions is going to be how many of your winning actions that you committed to do that week, have you done? This is just about measuring the actions done, not necessarily the results, because as I say, the results are going to lag behind; we will be looking at the results later, but we expect those to lag behind. What you need to keep doing is keep successfully implementing those winning action commitments that you've made.  If you complete a minimum of 85% of all the commitments you said you were going to do, then you're going to still be making positive progress towards your goals and spending your time intentionally as you planned.

Game time adjustments.

Let's be realistic, over a period of time you may find there are some actions you've planned that you've measured and feel you need to tweak. Just ensure you really have worked your plan before making changes to it. If you've measured and successfully implemented for 12 weeks and see that genuinely a change or adaptation of your planned actions is needed, then absolutely, revisit the exercise from chapter four, identify which actions will move you forward the most, identify the costs, willing to pay them? Great, you have a new winning action!

Remember; work the plan before you change the plan.

We are not in control

It may land somewhat paradoxically with you at first when I say that actually, ultimately we're not in control. The six steps in this book help support and empower us to get and stay clear about our true priorities and where we want to spend our most precious currency, our time. They help us get more of what matters to us done; sort the important from the time wasting or that which is just not aligned with our current priorities. However, there is so much beyond our control and no six step plan can change that. I hope this one helps you to respond more healthily and compassionately when something totally unexpected does come at you.

Whilst we spend time lovingly crafting a vision and goals, we need to acknowledge that life can throw us a curve ball at any time and we'll need to flex.

Do you have a faith or a spiritual practise? Rely on it, lean on it. My personal spiritual practice is 'Thank God for Jesus' and this I do both formally, as part of the circle of compassion with other like minded humans, and informally throughout each day, whether swimming in the sea, watching a sunset or waking in the middle of the night.

Many of us are raised to be extremely self sufficient. As adults, we find it very difficult, not only to ask for help, but accept help that's being offered. I think this sometimes goes for our spiritual practice too. We still feel the need to hold on to self-sufficiency and we don't see how this depletes us. Part of moving from feeling rushed, overwhelmed and always responsible to calm, clear and in control, has to be to acknowledge that, actually, we are not always in control, nor do we need to be. When we feel we must do eveything for everyone, it's no wonder we feel we can't cope; nobody can do everything for everyone! So, why do we find it so very hard to accept help?

I've worked with women who are so quick to help others but find it virtually impossible to allow that help to be reciprocated. I've been that woman. Sometimes, I still am, and I have to have a word with her for my own good and the good of those around me! We are constantly on the receiving end of the message that we *should* be able to do it all, so of course we feel there must be something wrong with us, that we're failing in some way, when we feel we can't.

But here's the secret. Nobody can do it all. Nobody can be all things to all people. And just because you see so many others around you trying to, doesn't mean it's ok. Remember I wrote earlier about the circle of compassion? We usually exclude ourselves from the circle of compassion. Yet, if we're trying to help another while standing outside that circle of compassion ourselves, it can come off as pretty condescending. Are we thinking well of ourselves because we're being so generous and giving while thinking nothing of our own needs? Are we denying we have the same needs as others? Setting ourselves up as some sort of super-human? That certainly doesn't give the other person an opportunity to reciprocate and may feel to them like receiving charity from you, rather than connectedness, friendship and kindness. When we include ourself in that circle of compassion, when we recognise we need to nurture ourself as well as others and fill our cup too, so we have something to pour out for others. We can be of service from a place of connection with others, of recognising we're all human, all struggling together, I have something of value to offer you and you have something of value to offer me. It makes it easier to receive compassion, help and support from others as well as to give it, when you recognise we're all in that circle together, you're not standing apart, somewhere higher, looking down at others from outside.

At the time of my husband's death as I described earlier in this book, this was a time in my life when I realised how not- self-sufficient I really was. I had been playing the part well, like many of us do, holding together the job, the home, the family, the exercise classes, the healthy lunchboxes, the permission slips for school trips, the Boden Kids catalogue orders, day trips, birthday parties, and on and on and on. But I was brought up short. I was forced to slam on the brakes and stop. And, at this time, I realised how very much I needed gentle compassion; from others, from myself and from my God.

I needed something bigger than myself.

Chapter Six. WASP.
Weekly Accountability & Support Power-up.

The vital importance of peer support.

Did you know, you're seven times more likely to sustain and lifestyle change you're trying to make, if you enlist peer support rather than try to go it alone? I've written a lot in the previous chapters about making it easier to do your winning actions than to not do them, and hands down the most proven way to stick to any new action, plan or change is to have support and accountability from a.n.other. This is why step six of The Method to Take Back Your Time is to WASP. To have a Weekly Accountability & Support Power-Up. It's why, when I run this book as a group course we meet together for 12 weeks in total, to not only learn the six steps but to provide one another Weekly Accountability and Support and a Power-up to keep everyone in the group embedding these changes and using The Method as the way they will manage their thinking, time and tasks from now on.

Seven times more likely to stick to changes with peer support.
In November 2004 speaking at a private conference at Rockefeller University, New York City,

Dr. Edward Miller, dean of the medical school and CEO of the hospital at Johns Hopkins University, described how, following life-saving surgeries such as coronary bypass graft or angioplasty, the bypass grafts often clog up within a few years; the angioplasties, in only a few months. In fact in fewer than 3 percent of the cases, do the surgeries, which initially give relief from pain, prevent the heart attacks the patients were heading toward or prolong their lives.

Knowing these grim statistics, doctors tell their patients: If you want to keep the pain from coming back, and if you don't want to have to repeat the surgery, and if you want to stop the course of your heart disease before it kills you, then you have to switch to a healthier lifestyle. You have to stop smoking, stop drinking, stop overeating, start exercising, and relieve your stress.

But very few do.

"If you look at people after coronary- artery bypass grafting two years later, ninety percent of them have not changed their lifestyle," Miller said. "And that's been studied over and over and over again. And so we're missing some link in there. Even though they know they have a very bad disease and they know they should change their lifestyle, for whatever reason, they can't."

Now, I wrote about finding your Purpose, vision and emotional rocket fuel, back in chapter two. I'd have thought having a purpose, a 'Big Why', like actually staying alive; preventing a heart attack, would be enough to make lifestyle changes, right? So why, even with that huge reason why, is it so difficult for people to make and sustain changes in lifestyle? To implement and carry through Winning Actions? And, what else can help us to do it?

Good news.

In 1993 Dr. Dean Ornish, a professor of medicine at the University of California at San Francisco, convinced the Mutual of Omaha insurance company to pay for an unusual experiment. The researchers recruited 194 patients who suffered from severely clogged arteries and could have bypass grafts or angioplasties covered by their insurance plans. Instead, they signed up for a trial. They were helped to quit smoking and switch to an extreme vegetarian diet that derived fewer than 10 percent of its calories from fat. They also took classes in meditation, relaxation, yoga, and aerobic exercise, which became parts of their daily routines and crucially, the patients got together for group conversations twice a week.

The program lasted for only a year. After that, they were on their own. But three years from the start, the study found, 77 percent of the patients had stuck with these lifestyle changes—and safely avoided the need for heart surgery. I think that's amazing news!

Without regular peer support, only one out of every ten people sustained these lifestyle changes, even in a crisis. With regular peer support, Dr. Ornish's team inspired and motivated seven out of ten of its heart patients to accomplish and sustain dramatic transformations. [10]

So, I'm going to end this book in the same way I started it. If you're serious about taking back your time, about making real changes in your life and moving from being a Rushing Woman to living in an Anti-Frantic way, then, as with any system, the strength and power of The Method to Take Back Your Time comes from implementing it in its entirety into your life, as your way of thinking, of making decisions, of managing your time. It's not one more thing to do, it's the way of getting things done. And, if you want those new ways to stick, you need to WASP.

It doesn't need to take long, depending on the size of the group you want to WASP with. I suggest each participant gets 5 to 7 minutes each and you can run it like a daily stand-up meeting. (Which, supposedly, were started by Queen Victoria who disliked meetings and realised they finished more quickly if she didn't invite people to sit!).

So, each of you in turn run through the following 5 questions together:
1. Did you connect to your vision & purpose last week?
2. What percentage of your planned action commitments did you complete last week?
3. What has changed for you as a result of those actions? (lead and lag indicators)
4. What might help you in the coming week? Any problems, stumbling blocks you foresee and want to ask support with? Or anything you want to kept accountable for?
5. Where do you feel you're currently at on the ECOC?

---

[10] Intensive lifestyle changes for reversal of coronary heart disease
Authors Dean Ornish, Larry W Scherwitz, James H Billings, K Lance Gould, Terri A Merritt, Stephen Sparler, William T Armstrong, Thomas A Ports, Richard L Kirkeeide, Charissa Hogeboom, Richard J Brand
Publication date 1998/12/16

Here's what some previous course participants have said:

*"Having those "check ins" scheduled weekly helps me keep myself accountable whilst sharing my experiences of how I have succeeded in taking back my time that week or maybe those times when I feel I could have practiced it better that week. Additionally, being able to offer advice or an alternative perspective to a colleague when they might need it."*

*"Each session has felt like a supportive and safe space to share and it's been reassuring to hear that others have the same struggles with maintaining a healthy work life balance when things get stressful"*

*"It's really enjoyable going through the course with other people – hearing their experiences and being held accountable is very motivating".*

*"Doing this alongside a great group of peers allowed me to see how others deal with similar problems and how we all can motivate one another to Take Back our Time".*

I'd like to leave you with the words of Nora McInerny again, "Imagine that moment when you slam on your brakes and stop just short of the bumper in front. That call you take where the bad news you never expected is delivered in a conversation that lasts just a few seconds. The birth of a child, everyone in the room waiting for that very first cry, the sound of life. The death of a loved one, the holy silence that follows that very last breath. These are moments that we do not rush to fill, that seem to quickly sort the chaos into manageable columns; that sort the real from the bullsh!t. They're only moments, quick visions of clarity before we're snapped back into the chaos. A moment of clarity I'd rather get without watching another loved one die".

Often, it is when we feel life has somehow 'given us a second chance' that it does suddenly matter to us, very much, to live a life based on our true priorities and purpose. I hope this book has blessed you. Thank you for reading it. I hope you implement it, and keep cycling through it, every 12 weeks and live the life you love, with the ones you love, in the way you love. Perhaps you might like to offer to lend this book to a friend? Perhaps you know someone who would like a copy for their birthday? Thank you for helping to spread the ideas and the blessings to create harmonious, intentional, purposeful lives, one rushing woman at a time.

Love,
Ellen x

Words of kindness

I recently enrolled on Ellen's time management course and it really was amazing.It is so much more than time management; we covered so many different topics and it has literally changed the way I think. I can highly recommend it to anyone thinking of doing this course, you won't be disappointed.

 Susan Mannion, small business owner at Style by Suze

I have just completed Ellen's time management 12 week course and have benefited so much from it. It's so much more than time management, offering a real insight into what drives us as well as exploring our goals and vision. Working with others in a group provided valuable support and encouragement and helped me keep on track. I know that I'm going to continue to manage my time much more effectively from now on.

 Caroline Snowden, Furniture Upcycler and Transformational Artist

This course has helped me find ways to feel happier by making small realistic changes to my lifestyle and I could not be more grateful for the difference it has made to my quality of life. The course has helped me to realise just how important it is to make appointments with myself and that it's OK to put me first sometimes.

 Steph

The workshops were a great opportunity to reflect on current life events understanding the impacts and how they present themselves in everyday situations. As someone who struggles to switch off, the course really highlighted the importance of setting boundaries and how to free up my time.

Alex G

I've thoroughly enjoyed working with Ellen on her 12 week course The Method to Take Back Your Time. I felt like Ellen really understood how I was self sabotaging. The method was an eye opener for me. Ellen gently guided us through the steps, we had time to reflect and her thoughtful questioning helped us identify how we could make things better. I feel I have the tools to be successful in any area of my life I choose to change.

Fiona Jones, Berkshire Lifestyle Concierge


I have recently completed Ellen's 12 week course The Method to Take Back Your Time and I have honestly been blown away by it. Like everyone who runs a small independent business I wear many hats and always need more time to get stuff done, the feeling of overwhelm can be enormous sometimes, but this course really highlighted just how much my business was impacting on other key areas in my life. Having fellow members on the course to discuss our actions with was incredibly helpful and supportive. I now have the tools to measure the change in how I think, tackle and prioritise my tasks. I've learned how to safeguard my health family and social time as Ellen helped me discover how to use my time more effectively so that I could enjoy the good things in life. I now feel empowered and back in control of my life/ work balance. I'm already seeing results.

Tee Stevenson, Owner and Director, Bloom and Bear


I can't thank Ellen enough, she has changed my whole thought process from negative to positive and has helped me go from feeling overwhelmed, as if I have no time, to feeling chilled, productive and as if I have more than enough time to fit everything in. I now feel super organised and I'm able to balance my time effectively between work and home life. Ellen has helped me stay focused and has helped me reach my goals over the last few months. I feel like a totally different person; having that little bit of 'me time' before doing everything helps so much, I've realised I *can* fit it all in! It's crazy how changing a few little things makes such a difference.

Lucy, Business Owner Aureille Aesthetics


Ellen has provided me with all the tools I need to achieve my vision. She has helped me recognise and then understand the various barriers along the way. I love the method, it has really worked. I now know what steps to take daily to live out that vision.

Rachel Tyrrell, Business Owner Cricketers Gin


I am a mother of four with a part time job and a fledgling business so time management is an issue. I have taken away so much from this course, in particular recognising the emotional cycle of change.

My daily planner has changed my life! I've gone from being a disorganised, stressed, mess to being in control of my time and recognising my boundaries. It helps me use my time intentionally and stops me from overbooking, I'm still busy but it's in a much more organised way now. Most of all I have taken away one simple sentence from Ellen that resets me every time I feel overwhelmed and that is, "what happens if nothing changes?" I can't thank you enough for the small but significant lifestyle changes you have encouraged me to make.

Kelly, Business Owner at Kelly Peel Aesthetics

Printed in Great Britain
by Amazon

28416496R00051